the chia cookbook

the chia cookbook

inventive, delicious recipes featuring nature's superfood

JANIE HOFFMAN

PHOTOGRAPHY BY Eric Wolfinger

TEN SPEED PRESS
Berkeley

Library of Congress Cataloging-in-Publication Data

Hoffman, Janie.
The Chia cookbook : inventive, delicious recipes featuring nature's superfood /
Janie Hoffman. – First edition.
pages cm
Summary: "Mamma Chia founder Janie Hoffman presents recipes for incorporating
superfood chia seeds into flavorful smoothies, snacks, meals, and desserts"– Provided by
publisher.
1. Chia. 2. Natural foods–Health aspects. 3. Cooking (Natural foods) I. Title.
TX558.C38H64 2014
641.3'02–dc23
2014005260

Trade Paperback ISBN: 978-1-60774-664-5
eBook ISBN: 978-1-60774-665-2

Printed in China

Design by Katy Brown
Food styling by Erin Quon

10 9 8 7 6 5 4 3 2 1

First Edition

This book is dedicated to all the beautiful souls spreading the love of chia and to my adventurous and delightful husband who joined me on this magical journey.

contents

acknowledgments

with gratitude & joy

There are so many beautiful souls that helped to bring this book to life.

With my deepest gratitude and joy:

To my delightful collaborator, Daryn Eller. Your beautiful and talented spirit is pure inspiration and I am blessed to have you by my side.

To Jackie Newgent, RDN, and Leslie Miller, your delicious and inventive contributions made us all better.

To my wonderful agent, Bonnie Solow. Thank you for always being there to lend your wise counsel.

To Lisa Westmoreland, my fantastic senior editor at Ten Speed Press. I am eternally grateful for your reaching out and supporting this project every step of the way.

To the rest of the amazing team who helped create this book: designer Katy Brown, photographer Eric Wolfinger, and publicists Natalie Mulford and Erin Welke.

To all the organic farmers around the world. Your care of the land and our food feeds both the soul of humanity and the soul of the planet.

Big thank-you to my friends who have supported and inspired me on my journey, especially Jeanne Christiansen; Ariana Garrett; Peter and Linda Gevorkian; Wendy Gilleland; Frank and Theresa Golbeck; Stacy, David, Lev, and Shayna Grossman; Robert Helgeson Jr.; John and Ami Ken; Jackie Townsend Konstanturos; Jim Lieb; Laura and Jay Lieberman; Steven and Ellen Osinski; Jamie Phillips; Gerry Ransom; Karen and John Roberts; Dale Rodriguez; Nancy Rosenzweig; Woody Tasch; Rob Thomas; Grace Venus; Mary Waldner; Bill Weiland; and Ruth and Stanley Westreich.

Heaps of gratitude to all the dedicated and talented souls on the Mamma Chia team, past and present. This really is a team sport and I am blessed to share this adventure with you. Thank you!

Love and gratitude to the beautiful Mamma Chia community. Thank you so much for taking this ride with us and helping us spread the love of chia.

To my family: Kathleen and Donald Flynn; Katie and Jeff Harvey; Jim and Barb Hawkins; Audrey and Dave Hoffman; Bruce, Donna, Marisa, Nick, and Sean Hoffman; and the wonderful O'Connell clan. Your love is deeply appreciated.

To Lance, your love and kindness inspires me daily. I am so grateful for your unwavering support and friendship. I love you so!

preface

The first time I heard about chia seeds, I had more than just
a casual interest in learning about new foods with health-enhancing powers.
I was born a very healthy, vibrant soul who approached life with a lot of gusto
when, during my early twenties, I was hit hard with several different autoimmune disorders. Gradually, after a lot of trial and error, I learned that what
I chose to eat had a significant impact on how I felt.

This challenging journey into illness started with a skin and muscle disease
called dermatomyositis, then advanced to include chronic fatigue, lupus, and
scleroderma, a hardening and contraction of the skin and connective tissue.
At times my muscles were so weak, I couldn't even dress myself. I developed
severe rashes and hair loss, too. Chemotherapy and steroids were prescribed
and I dutifully complied with my doctor's orders, only to find that, for me at least,
the drugs had more side effects than benefits. Needless to say, it was rough.

And yet I knew there must be a solution. So I tried strict vegetarian and
macrobiotic diets (to no avail); studied meditation and yoga and dedicated
myself to service to humanity and the planet (all of which seemed to help on
many levels); and, finally, decided to eat only organic whole foods whenever
possible. The last one proved to be the tipping point and, although I continued

to have flare-ups, I did experience much better health. I still wasn't completely well, but I was very grateful for how far I'd come.

That's where things stood when, almost by happenstance, I learned about chia, minuscule seeds in the mint family with an astonishing amount of omega-3s, protein, fiber, calcium, antioxidants—and more—packed within their tiny shells. My friend Wendy mentioned chia one day when we were working out and, prompted by her enthusiasm, I went home and did a little research. Could the seeds really have as many nutrients as she said? (Yes!) Did the Aztecs really power their conquests with chia seeds? (History tells us so!) How could I not give chia a try? And I'll be forever thankful that I did: the bag of chia seeds that arrived on my doorstep a few days later absolutely changed my life.

I started by consuming just a few tablespoons of seeds a day, and right away felt a difference in my stamina and energy levels. Suddenly, I was filled with more vitality than I could ever have imagined. All those years of grappling with my health taught me to listen closely to my body, and I just knew that the chia was having a *significant* effect. Within a few months, I became 100 percent symptom free and have remained so ever since. I don't even test positive for autoimmune disorders anymore.

When I saw all that this amazing seed could do, I wanted to shout it from the rooftops, letting everyone know about chia. I went into my kitchen and experimented, trying to create chia-based meals, drinks, and snacks that I could share with friends and family. I baked with chia. Made salads with chia. Worked the seeds into my husband's turkey burgers. Added them to salsas and ketchups and mustards. Used them to whip up puddings and smoothies. I made a variety of blended juice beverages with them, too, and began sharing them at parties and yoga classes. "Wouldn't this all work nicely into a chia cookbook?" I thought to myself. "What a great way to let people know about this incredible seed." I turned to my dear friend Ariana, one of the best and most intuitive cooks I know, and asked her if she'd like to collaborate on a cookbook. She enthusiastically agreed—she too had fallen in love with my chia creations—but the next day, she realized there was no way to work it into her schedule.

Left to my own devices, I came up with another way to spread the love of chia: Mamma Chia, the organic chia-based food and beverage company I founded in 2009. I had no prior experience in the food or beverage business, so taking all those chia drinks and edibles I'd been concocting in my home kitchen and turning them into marketable products was a huge leap of faith. But I felt strongly that I needed to share chia with the world and, to my never-ending delight, the Mamma Chia Vitality Beverage, our first product—and the first chia drink ever to hit the market—made it into stores and immediately started flying off the shelves. Mamma Chia has gone on to win numerous awards and continues to develop new products. And just as Mamma Chia has grown, so have the number of chia devotees. The chia renaissance is definitely on!

It fills me with so much joy and gratitude to know there are rapidly growing throngs of fellow chia lovers. Yet even though the seeds are everywhere now (not just stashed on some dusty shelf in the back of a health food store like they used to be), too few people are aware of what a fantastic ingredient chia is to have in your culinary arsenal. Sure, you can just sprinkle the seeds on your food and automatically give it a healthier luster. But that would be missing the boat (and the fun). Chia can provide hearty dishes with a pleasing bit of crunch, turn soups creamy (without the cream), put a fresh spin on one-pot meals, make cocktail party–worthy drinks look gorgeous, and keep traditional baked goods light and moist. When you know how to cook with chia, the possibilities are endless.

Timing can be everything. If I hadn't been forced to put aside my longing to create a chia cookbook, Mamma Chia never would have been born, so I'm incredibly thankful that Ariana was so busy. (And she lovingly reminds me that turning down the cookbook collaboration was one of the best acts of friendship she could have ever performed.) But now with the company up and running, I present, at long last, *The Chia Cookbook*. I think you'll be surprised at just how versatile and easy to use the seeds are, and amazed at how full of vitality they make you feel. This is where healthiness and happiness meet.

chia basics

If you could wave a magic wand and change every meal you eat into a supernutritious, disease-fighting, energy-raising, terrific-tasting feast, you'd do it, wouldn't you? Of course you would! Well, consider this: you don't need a magic wand to capture all that goodness, just the magic of chia. Packed within these tiny seeds are enough omega-3s, protein, fiber, antioxidants, calcium, and other important minerals to give any dish a substantial health boost. But that's not all. Chia has unique characteristics that make it a dream ingredient. Just a few tablespoons of the seeds have the potential to transform the texture, lower the calorie count, and enhance the visual appeal of a recipe. Cook with chia and you'll not only get the benefits of this nutritional power-house, you'll also delight in sumptuous, flavorful, satisfying food.

the chia story

Chia is nearly ubiquitous now. You can find it in almost every market (or at least every enlightened one), and it's easily ordered online. But for a long time most of us lived in what you might call a chia desert: the seeds were primarily used in Latin American countries, and even there they were often something of an afterthought. Once upon a time, though, chia was the food of warrior kings.

Some historians believe chia may have been used for food as early as 3500 BCE, and we know for sure that it was widely cultivated in Mexico as well as South and Central America long before Columbus's arrival. California Indians were chia enthusiasts, too. Most famously, though, chia was beloved by the Aztecs. Members of this advanced civilization cultivated the seeds with sophisticated farming methods, then combined them with grains to create flour, used them to make porridge, and stirred them into water to whip up a superhydrating drink. The Aztecs also relied on chia to treat gastrointestinal and respiratory ills, fever, and burns. The seeds were used to pay taxes and as a spiritual offering to the gods, too. But what gives us the biggest clue to chia's transformative powers is the fact that Aztec warriors carried little bags of seeds with them for stamina as they went into battle. Chia is *that* energizing. Even today, the Tarahumara Indians, who live in the remote Copper Canyon in Mexico and are known as the best long-distance runners in the world, use chia to sustain them on their epic 100-plus-mile runs.

After the Spanish conquered the Aztecs and decimated their crops, chia survived (barely) only as a regional specialty in parts of Mexico, Guatemala, and other Latin American countries. Except for fans of the funny, sprouting ceramic Chia Pets, few people in the United States or elsewhere had even heard of the seeds, let alone considered eating them. So chia was ripe for rediscovery—and that's exactly what happened when a group of agriculture scientists searching for new crops began investigating the nutritional properties of chia. What they discovered—and subsequently revealed to the world—was undoubtedly what the Aztecs knew all along: chia is loaded with just about everything a body needs for energy, healing, and good health.

When I first started reading up on chia, I was particularly wowed by the seeds' omega-3 content. As you may already know, the benefits of omega-3s are exponential. Not only have these fatty acids been shown to reduce inflammation and lower the incidence of its associated ills—heart disease, diabetes, and Alzheimer's among them—omega-3s may also decrease the risk of cancer, slow aging, improve brain function, and, of great interest to me, help diminish symptoms of autoimmune disease.

Omega-3s, though, are just part of chia's extraordinary package of nutrients. About 23 percent of each chia seed is made up of protein, and 33 to 38 percent is comprised of fiber. Chia is also rich in the minerals calcium and iron, and it's a great source of antioxidants, particularly a type of antioxidant called "phenols," which are known to have cardioprotective and anti-inflammatory effects. You can see why this is a seed that nutritionists can (and do) get behind. So do people who have concerns about gluten and genetically modified foods: chia is naturally gluten-free and non-GMO. (For more on chia's health benefits, see page 4.)

cooking with chia

Chia may look a little like other seeds in your spice rack or cabinet, but it's best to think about this member of the mint family (its botanical name is *Salvia hispanica*) as a food rather than a garnish or flavoring. In fact, chia is a *whole food*—and its qualities are distinctly different from anything else in your cupboard. Unlike flaxseeds, for instance, chia doesn't need to be ground to release its nutrients—both the ground and whole seeds are equal in nutrients. Their flavor is also much milder than that of flaxseeds. Chia, in fact, is chameleonlike: the seeds take on the flavor of whatever you pair them with.

just how good for you is chia? very!

If you're looking to maximize the protective and healing power of your diet, you can't do better than to cook with chia. It comes by its superfood status honestly: gram for gram, the seeds have 70 percent more protein than soybeans, 25 percent more fiber than flaxseed, 600 percent more calcium than milk, 200 percent more potassium than a banana, and 30 percent more antioxidants than blueberries.

The omega-3 content of chia is particularly striking. Chia, like all plant sources of the fatty acids, contains a type of omega-3 called alpha-linolenic acid (ALA). Some ALA is converted by the body to fatty acids called DHA and EPA, the same omega-3s contained in fish and which we know confer so many health benefits. ALA also has benefits of its own, especially when it comes to lowering the risk of cardiovascular disease.

Now that the popularity of chia has exploded, researchers are beginning to turn their attention to the seeds' effect on health. And the results are already promising. For instance, in 2007, Canadian researchers had twenty men and women consume 37 grams of Salba (a name brand form of chia) daily for twelve weeks. All of the study participants had diabetes, which put them at risk for heart disease. By the end of the study, the chia-eaters lowered their blood pressure and levels of CRP, a marker of inflammation—an indication that they had reduced their risk of heart disease. (On the contrary, when the same subjects tried consuming 37 grams of wheat bran a day for the same period of time, it did not have the same effect.)

I wasn't too surprised by the results of that study. While I'm not someone who believes in magic bullets, I know I'm living proof that, when combined with other nutritious whole foods and a healthy lifestyle, chia can substantially improve your energy and well-being. Here's what it has to offer.

Chia's Nutritional Profile

Nutrient	Per 1 ounce (about 2 tablespoons)
Calories	138
Protein	4.7 grams
Fat (the source of chia's omegas)	8.7 grams
Omega-3s	5.1 grams
Omega-6s	1.6 grams
Omega-9s	0.6 grams
Carbohydrate	11.9 grams
Fiber	9.8 grams
Calcium	179 milligrams
Iron	2.2 milligrams
Magnesium	95 milligrams
Phosphorus	244 milligrams
Potassium	115 milligrams
Zinc	1.3 milligrams
Copper	0.3 milligrams
Vitamin C	0.5 milligrams
Thiamin	0.2 milligrams
Riboflavin	0.05 milligrams
Niacin	2.5 milligrams
Folate	14 micrograms
Vitamin A	15 International Units (IU)
Vitamin E	0.1 mg

Source: US Department of Agriculture (USDA) National
Nutrient Database for Standard Reference.

Chia can also transform the texture and look of a dish. When you stir the whole seeds into food, they impart a satisfying bit of crunch. Yet soak chia in liquid before combining it with other ingredients and it will create a gel that adds moisture, thickness, and a velvety mouthfeel to a dish. In the same vein, when you add dry chia to a food that's very moist and liquidy—yogurt, for example—the seeds will absorb some of the liquid and gel up a bit (how much depends on how wet the food is you're adding them to and how long they sit before the food is eaten). Many of the recipes in this book call for chia gel, which is made simply by whisking the seeds into water or other liquid and letting it sit for about 20 minutes. The gel can be used to replace eggs in baking, make puddings without milk or cream, and give body to salad dressings (while also reducing the amount of oil needed). And that's just scratching the surface—chia is much more than just your average pantry staple! I'm hard-pressed to think of anything with its combination of culinary range and nutritional value.

types of chia

Chia seeds come in both black and white varieties, which lets you play with the aesthetics of whatever you're making while still giving it the same healthy boost. I love the freckled appearance of black seeds in some dishes while in others—say, in recipes with very light-colored ingredients—I prefer the incognito effect of white seeds. (Black seeds can go nearly undercover, too, when you use them in dark-colored foods like chocolate cookies.) You can also buy preground seeds. Known as "milled" chia, it has the same nutritional qualities as whole seeds and works well when you don't want crunch or viscosity or the appearance of seeds. For the most part, when you stir milled chia into a dish, it flies completely under the radar while adding texture and absorbing moisture at the same time.

the slimming side effects of chia

When it comes to helping you lose weight, chia has a few things going for it. One is that its capacity for absorbing water makes you feel full without substantially driving up your day's calorie count. Chia, in fact, absorbs about *ten* times its weight in liquid, so while the seeds may be tiny, they hydrate in your stomach, taking up space and preventing hunger. (Chia gel, which is already hydrated, does the same.) The seeds' high protein and fiber content may be another reason some people have shed pounds with chia. Studies show that both protein and fiber lead to increased satiety and reduced calorie intake. Some people have found that taking two tablespoons of chia stirred into water after breakfast and again after lunch helps them have fewer cravings and eat fewer calories throughout the day.

Finally, because chia adds viscosity to food, cooking with the seeds allows you to cut down on unhealthy fat calories. Just think of it: silky, "creamy" puddings without cream; salad dressings with less oil; shakes without ice cream. That's a yummy way to slim down and still feel satisfied.

the recipes

As you read through the recipes in this book, you'll see that it's possible to incorporate chia into everything, and I mean *everything*—breakfast foods, soups, salads, cocktails, main dishes, desserts. The seeds also complement all epicurean traditions. I've had the good fortune to travel to many beautiful countries all over the world. I even lived in Hong Kong for a time and now reside about an hour from Mexico. This has given me a taste for the food of many cultures, and you'll see that multiculturalism reflected in the book's collection of varied dishes.

I lead a busy life and I'm sure you do, too, so these recipes are also designed to be quick and easy. There's no special equipment required—using a blender and food processor is about as fancy as it gets—and the ingredients are easy to find. You shouldn't have to spend a lot of time and money or slave over a stove to work nutritious, delicious food into your life, and with these dishes, you won't have to.

My goal has always been to expand the community of chia aficionados. When you're on to a good thing, why not share it? Now you can also be part of the chia love train. Use this book not only to treat yourself to food that tastes terrific and boosts your well-being but also to indulge and nourish your family and friends. They'll thank you with every delectable, delightful bite.

chia fundamentals: from choosing to using

Everything from sourcing and storing chia to working it into a dish is very, very simple—a snap. Here are the details.

SELECTING CHIA
For the most versatility, I recommend that you have both black and white chia seeds on hand. Most recipes call for using one color or the other, or give you a choice between the two, but consider it a suggestion. You should feel free

to choose whichever shade you prefer or to even mix them if you like (there is no taste difference). Some recipes utilize milled chia, which combines well with flour and makes a good flour substitute itself, so have that in your pantry as well—or simply grind the whole seeds on your own as needed using a spice meal or clean coffee grinder.

There are a couple of other types of chia on the market as well. Chia oil is essentially concentrated omega-3s, though it comes to you without the seeds' fiber and protein. The oil is mild tasting and is generally used in salad dressings and baking. Chia bran is a form of chia with the omega-3 fatty acids removed and the fiber and protein left intact. I don't use either in this book or at home—I'm personally a fan of the whole chia seed with its complete package of nutrients—but if you're interested in experimenting, it's nice to know there are several chia options.

Chia is primarily a tropical or subtropical crop, so most of the seeds you'll find on the market come from Mexico, Central and South America, or Australia. I love to buy locally, and generally do, but one of the foods I make an exception for is chia. What I'm firm on, though, is buying USDA certified organic chia. Chia isn't a particularly pesticide-ridden product. Because of its antioxidants, it's mostly resistant to pests if grown in its native lands, so many growers in Mexico and Central America don't use pesticides. However, most of the nonorganic growers do use herbicides and synthetic fertilizers, and since I've found I'm sensitive to chemicals (and I believe Mother Earth is, too), I opt for certified organic. Organic chia can be slightly more expensive (although not always), but if it fits into your budget, look for the USDA organic seal on the package to know you're getting the real thing. I think the benefits of organic are well worth any extra cost, and at Mamma Chia, it's what we've chosen to sell ourselves: we offer USDA certified organic bagged chia, as well as certified organic chia beverages and snacks (www.mammachia.com).

BUYING CHIA

Chia is generally sold in bags or pouches in sizes ranging from a half pound to three pounds. Some grocery stores make it available in bulk bins as well. Unlike a few years back when rooting out the seeds was like trick-or-treating in a neighborhood where nobody is home, it's now pretty easy to find chia at your local supermarket—or even your local big box store. Natural foods stores tend to offer the most varieties of chia, but what you can't find in your local grocery can be easily accessed online.

STORING CHIA

Remember how I said everything about chia is simple? That includes storing it. You can basically just empty it into a jar (or leave it in its resealable pouch), place it in a cool, dry place, and not worry about it ever going bad. (And I mean practically ever—archaeologists have found chia seeds that survived hundreds of years without deteriorating.) As a lover of all things chia, I think the seeds are beautiful (check them out up close—they have a magical marbling design) and look wonderful displayed in glass jars or even in open bowls. I keep some of mine on my kitchen counter in two interlocking dishes in the shape of a yin-yang symbol. One bowl holds white chia, the other, black. Not only are they aesthetically delightful, it's great to have the seeds so close at hand while I'm cooking.

chia tips and tricks

The recipes in this book are designed to leave nothing to chance. In other words, you don't need to have tremendous "chia skills" to make each of them a success. That said, learning what happens to the seeds when you combine them with other ingredients will give you insight into how the recipes work—as well as familiarize you with the techniques needed to incorporate chia into dishes and drinks you already make on a regular basis. My hope is that you'll be inspired to create many yummy chia recipes of your own.

how much chia to use

The amount of chia called for in each dish in this book was calculated to achieve the best balance of ingredients. When you're adding chia to a recipe you already have, start with a tablespoon, test, and add more as needed. You might, for instance, add a tablespoon of whole seeds per serving to a grain salad, then taste a spoonful to see if the texture is right. When adding chia gel to, say, a smoothie, start by adding a half cup, then test out the viscosity. You can always add more.

In order to reap the considerable health benefits of chia, try to get in a total intake of about one or two tablespoons a day. As yet, no one has come up with an RDA (recommended dietary allowance) for chia, but in addition to listening to our bodies—they are so wise, after all—we can also look to the RDA for alpha-linolenic acid for some guidance. ALA, as explained on page 4, is the type of omega-3 fatty acid contained in chia. The US Department of Agriculture's RDA for ALA is 1.1 grams for women and 1.6 grams for men daily. One tablespoon of chia has about 2.3 grams of ALA, double the RDA, but it's also safe. I personally average two to four tablespoons of chia a day, the amount I've found to be most therapeutic.

chia as a flour substitute

Milled chia has a flourlike consistency that makes it a great substitute for all-purpose white flour in all kinds of recipes. Swap milled chia for flour to thicken soups, mix it with bread crumbs to create a coating for breaded fish or chicken, and use it as a flour replacement in baking. A good rule of thumb in baking: Replace up to one-quarter of the flour called for in a recipe with milled chia. Doing so will give your baked goods an automatic health upgrade, raising their fiber by a factor of eleven, while nicely upping their protein and omega-3 content, too.

CHIA EGG SUBSTITUTE

To replace one large egg, combine one tablespoon chia seeds with three table-spoons of room-temperature purified water. Whisk and let sit until the gel forms, about 20 minutes.

Note that chia adds water to a recipe, so if you're using the gel as an egg substitute in baking, your baked goods may turn out slightly moister than they would if you were using eggs. If you're aiming for a drier texture, simply add a few minutes to the baking time to allow the excess liquid to evaporate.

chia as an egg substitute

When chia is hydrated to the right consistency, it forms a gel that's as thick and smooth as an egg. That makes chia a perfect egg replacement in baking as well as an excellent egg "extender" for dishes like frittatas and omelets. For instance, in a frittata recipe calling for four eggs, you can substitute one of them for a portion of chia egg substitute (see above), reducing the amount of saturated fat in the dish. It's also just nice to know that if you find yourself short of eggs while in the middle of cooking, chia can fill in—no need to stop what you're doing and run out to the store.

getting chia drinks just right

Most of the smoothies, shakes, and cocktails in this book call for creating a chia gel that's later added to other ingredients. There's a reason for that. When chia seeds are fully hydrated, they won't cause further thickening to the beverage you add them to. Dry seeds, on the other hand, can turn a drink thicker than you'd like it to be. For best results use chia gel, not dry seeds, in smoothies, shakes, and cocktails.

a chia gel primer

The first time people come across chia, they are often surprised by its hydrophilic properties. Chia, that is, absorbs water—about ten times its weight in water, in fact. Drop a tiny seed on a wet kitchen counter and it will suddenly develop a gel coating that's a lot like Jell-O. That jellylike substance enveloping the seed is the release of soluble fiber, and it happens to make a very handy (and healthy) thickening agent known as "chia gel."

The thickness of a chia gel depends on how much liquid you mix the seeds with. I always have several jars of chia gel of varying viscosity in my refrigerator because some recipes work best with a thin gel while others work better with a very thick one. Naturally, it just depends on what you're making. You don't have to worry about tinkering with viscosity when using this book—all the recipes that incorporate chia gel give instructions on how to make the right one for that dish. But if you'd like to have some chia gel on hand for other uses—and I recommend that you do!—it couldn't be easier to make.

One of my favorite ways to use the gel is in condiments and salad dressings. Cutting ketchup, mustard, mayonnaise, salsa, guacamole, relish, and vinaigrettes with chia will make them go farther, increase their nutrients, and cut their fat and calorie content. By adding volume to "doctored" condiments and dressings, chia gel can also help you consume less sugar, a common ingredient in many prepared foods. A thick gel generally works best and at a ratio of about one-third gel to two-thirds condiment or dressing.

Here are two chia gel recipes, plus some tips to net you the best results.

FOR A STELLAR GEL

- Think beyond water. Using juice, broth, or almond, coconut, or some other type of milk to hydrate the chia will impart more flavor to whatever dish you add the gel to.
- Take the instruction to use liquids at room temperature seriously. Cold liquids can make the gelling process take much longer.

- While the texture of the chia will change as you turn it into a gel, the color won't. If you don't want to see the seeds in the food you're adding it to, use white or black depending on the main ingredients of the dish (for example, white chia paired with rice and black chia paired with black beans).
- It usually takes about 20 minutes for chia to gel properly. When in doubt about whether the mixture has sat long enough, err on the side of adding more time. For the most part, the crunch goes out of the seeds as they hydrate, but if you like a very smooth texture, try letting the mixture sit a little longer than 20 minutes. Additional whisking will also help prevent lumping and keep the gel smooth.
- Experiment. There's no law that says you must use only the thin or thick gel. Try out different viscosities to see what suits your preferences and recipe best.

THIN CHIA GEL

Best for smoothies, cocktails, soups

Whisk together 1 cup of room-temperature purified water and 2 tablespoons of black or white chia seeds. Let stand for at least 20 minutes. The mixture may need additional whisking to prevent clumping. Use immediately or store well covered in the refrigerator for up to 1 week.

THICK CHIA GEL

Best for condiments, dips, salad dressings, sauces, egg dishes

Follow the directions above using 3 tablespoons of room-temperature purified water and 1 tablespoon of black or white chia seeds.

more ways to use chia

Chia is a cook's dream ingredient—but you don't always have to cook to enjoy it. Chia works with just about everything as a topping or mix-in, so think of adding it to all kinds of dishes and snacks—it's an effortless way to get a lot more nutrients into your diet. I even carry a little eco-friendly snack bag of the seeds with me at all times so I have chia at the ready when I'm eating out. A few ways to use it: Sprinkle a teaspoon or two on top of a salad to give it a nice bit of crunch. Whisk chia into a carton of yogurt or sprinkle the seeds on ice cream. Add chia to condiments (see page 14), scatter seeds atop nut butters in a sandwich, or stir it into a stir-fry or pasta sauce. Dust the top of a frosted carrot cake with seeds, spread some on top of a bagel with cream cheese, add a spoonful to a bowl of soup right before eating, or mix them into a bowlful of bran flakes. There's really nowhere chia seeds can't go!

One note of interest: Because of chia's unique properties, you have to play around with it to find the exact texture you like. For instance, some people like to add chia to yogurt and let it sit for a while, letting the seeds gel up and soften. Others like the crunch and eat their seeded yogurt right away. It's all a matter of personal preference, and experience will teach you what you like best.

the chia pantry

Even if you consume chia all by itself—I occasionally pop a handful of chia seeds into my mouth all by themselves, while my hubby, Lance, does a shot (one tablespoon) of raw whole seeds in the morning—you are sure to benefit from the seeds' extraordinary collection of nutrients. I'm convinced that a few tablespoons a day can indeed help to keep the doctor away! But, that said, pairing chia with other healthy foods has always made the most sense to me. And I believe that nothing promotes well-being as effectively as the combination of chia and fresh organic produce, whole grains, and healthy sources of protein. It was this team of natural, unprocessed foods—with chia playing quarterback—that helped me finally work my way back to good health after suffering from multiple autoimmune diseases for twenty years.

As you prepare to make the recipes in this book, you'll be stocking your pantry with those same nutritious ingredients. Most of them need no introduction; some, though, may be new to you or need some clarification. What follows are the particulars on selected ingredients (if you missed the most important particulars—those on chia—they begin back on page 3), plus some overriding principles I use when stocking my own kitchen.

ORGANIC

A big part of my road to recovery was paved with organic foods. So I'm a big proponent of enjoying food—and supporting the farmers who grow it—that is cultivated without the use of synthetic fertilizers, pesticides, herbicides, sewage sludge, irradiation, and genetic engineering. That is all stuff our bodies and Mother Earth don't need! When buying meat, poultry, eggs, and dairy, I vote for choosing animal products that are free of antibiotics and growth hormones, and, also important, raised humanely.

I don't add the word "organic" in front of every ingredient in this book, but consider it implied—I do recommend seeking out organic ingredients whenever possible. Organic food is sometimes (but not always) more expensive than conventional foods and is not always available or convenient, so just do the best you can. Keep in mind, too, that some farmers are producing sustainable (or no-spray) fruits and vegetables and raising their animals humanely, but may not have gone through the expensive and time-consuming process of getting organically certified. When you shop at your local farmers' market (more on that below), ask the farmers how they produce their food. You may have more options than you're aware of.

SEASONAL AND LOCALLY SOURCED

If you have a farmers' market in your area (and new ones are popping up all the time), you are in luck. Farmers' markets are a joy! Not only do they provide a heady experience—all those piles of beautiful fruits and vegetables—they give you the opportunity to buy local, seasonal food produced right in your own backyard. That means it hasn't been flown or trucked in from some faraway spot, losing nutrients and flavor in transit while also contributing to air pollution. Farmers who sell their in-season produce at local markets are able to allow it to ripen on the vine, ensuring better flavor. You only have to look at and taste the difference between a summer tomato and a winter one to know that eating seasonally is the way to go.

These days "buy local" might seem like a trendy phrase, but I heartily believe in the sentiment. Besides supporting the small farmers and businesses that add humanity to our communities, buying from local farms helps keep our planet healthy and vital. And buying local and shopping at farmers' markets is the best way to guarantee you get the most nutritious, yummiest food possible. Can't make it to the market? Consider having farmers' goods delivered right to your door (or a convenient pickup spot) through Community Supported Agriculture (CSA). Belonging to a CSA is like belonging to a co-op—you have a stake in the farm. For information on farmers' markets in your neck of the woods or having organic produce delivered right to your door or a pickup spot, check out www.localharvest.org.

Not everything, of course, can be sourced locally (chia is an example of that), but you can take comfort in knowing that many companies that sell food nationwide are working to be conscientious members of their local communities. I'm a founding member of Slow Money, a nonprofit organization and movement with local chapters across the country that are helping to build communities and support the local food movement. (For more information, visit http://slowmoney.org.) From my work in the trenches, I'm happy to report that more and more individuals and companies are working to change the food-supply landscape for the better.

NON-GMO

GMO stands for "genetically modified organisms" and refers to plants or animals that have been created by inserting the DNA of one species into another. What are the repercussions of producing foods that cannot occur in nature or be generated through traditional crossbreeding techniques? The problem is we don't really know, although we have some clues. One purpose for tampering with the DNA of certain crops is to make them resistant to herbicides, thereby killing invasive weeds but leaving the crop intact. Yet that means that GMOs have the potential to contain even more chemical residue than usual. It's also possible that GMOs will contain allergens that the plants ordinarily wouldn't have (a dangerous surprise if you happen to react to those allergens), and that they will disrupt local ecosystems.

Given the uncertain impact of GMOs, I always try to avoid foods that have a good chance of being genetically modified or opt for organic versions (foods must be non-GMO to earn a USDA certified organic seal). The most common GMO edible crops are canola, corn, papaya, soybeans, sugar beets, zucchini, and yellow summer squash. You'll see that I don't use canola oil in this book, and, as for the other foods on the list, I recommend that you go organic or with varieties that specifically are non-GMO. There's no national law that says genetically modified foods must be labeled in the United States, but some companies (and Mamma Chia is one of them) have their products certified non-GMO by third-party agencies. Look for a non-GMO seal on the product labels.

notes on selected ingredients

You'll find these ingredients used throughout the book. None of them are difficult to find and they'll make a healthy addition to your larder.

AVOCADO This ingredient is close to my heart—I live on an avocado farm. All the recipes in this book specify Hass avocados, and they're truly the tastiest variety. Avocados are ready to use when the fruit gives way to gentle but firm pressure as you press a finger into the skin. Don't worry about taking home a rock-hard avocado from the market; it will soften up after a few days. Once it hits the ripe stage (allow the skin to get dark but not pucker), then it can be stored in the refrigerator until you're ready to use it. Always store leftover avocado with the seed in and the flesh covered—eco-friendly, reusable bags (such as neat-os, which can be found at http://neat-os.com) work great.

FRUIT JUICE Juice is integral to the flavor of the chia smoothies and cocktails in this book. Whenever possible, choose fresh juices and if you use bottled ones, try to find those that do not have added sugars or preservatives.

OILS My go-to oil is organic extra-virgin olive oil and you'll find it used throughout. Olive oil flavors run the gamut from peppery to mild; choose whichever one suits your personal taste. Extra-virgin olive oil will begin to smoke if you use it over too high heat, though it's ideal for the low- and medium-heat cooking called for in this book. Other oils used in this book (though only in one recipe, the Serrano Pineapple-Papaya Smoothie, page 26) are pistachio and avocado. These are also excellent used in salads or drizzled over fish, chicken, or grilled vegetables. Try these healthy oils as a replacement in dishes like the Overnight Caprese Baked Egg (page 50) or Truffle Cauliflower "Popcorn" with Chia Seeds (page 65). Avocado oil— specifically, expeller-pressed, naturally refined avocado oil—also has a high smoke point, so consider using it for recipes that call for high heat or lengthy preparations using medium-high heat.

VINEGARS Vinegar brightens up and balances the flavors of just about any dish. Stock your pantry with balsamic vinegars, both white and red (white is preferable when you're using other ingredients—mozzarella, for instance—that may be "stained" by the red), and the more mellow-tasting brown rice vinegar. I choose the brown rice vinegar over regular rice vinegar because many of the latter are processed with chemicals rather than fermented naturally. When buying apple cider vinegar, look for those that are slightly cloudy. This means they're unfiltered and contain the "mother"—a compound created during fermentation—and have more enzymes and minerals than filtered vinegars.

SWEETENERS You'll notice that the recipes in this book contain very little sugar, and no refined sugar. Instead, you'll need to have agave, honey, maple syrup, and coconut or date palm sugar on hand. These natural sweeteners have more health-promoting properties than refined sugar and are less likely to cause rapid rises—and crashes—in blood sugar. While agave can be found in most natural foods stores (and many supermarkets), I recommend buying honey and maple syrup from local purveyors if it's produced in your area. (I always buy organic over nonorganic; the one exception is local honey and maple syrup—if I can get them, I'll choose them over organic varieties produced far away.) Coconut and date palm sugars are just now beginning to make their way into stores. Look for them at natural foods groceries, online, and in Asian markets.

NONDAIRY MILKS In most cases, I prefer to use nondairy milks (only a few recipes in the book call for dairy milk products). I'm amazed at the array of them now available on grocery store shelves. For these recipes, I chose the ones I typically use at home and that I think work best: almond milk and coconut milk. But hemp milk, soy milk (be sure it's non-GMO), and rice milk will all work well, too.

YOGURT Whenever yogurt—Greek, Icelandic, or otherwise—is called for in a recipe, the level of fatness (non, low, or full) is left up to you.

AMINOS I've long been a fan of Bragg's Liquid Aminos, which adds a hint of saltiness to food along with 16 amino acids, the building blocks of protein. Although it's made from soy, it's certified non-GMO, and a healthy substitute for soy sauce. Recently, I came across Coconut Secret's Coconut Aminos, a good alternative if you have a soy allergy. Both are available in natural foods stores. (Bragg's is also sold in many traditional supermarkets.)

MEATS AND FISH I don't eat much meat, but when I do I try my best to buy from producers whose animals are organically and/or grass fed and raised humanely without antibiotics or added hormones. It's not always easy to find these healthier meats (and by healthy, I mean healthy for our bodies and the planet), but many suppliers sell at farmers' markets and at natural foods stores. I also try to be a conscientious seafood consumer. If you're like-minded, the Monterey Bay Aquarium Seafood Watch program lets you stay in touch with the latest on which fish are safe and caught through sustainable fishing practices (www.seafoodwatch.org/cr/seafoodwatch.aspx).

tools and equipment

If you have on hand the usual assortment of pots and pans, plus a blender and food processor, then you're all set to make these recipes. There's nothing fancy required. You'll notice that when the need for a nonstick skillet arises, I recommend using ones that are PFOA-free. PFOA stands for perfluorooctanoic acid, a chemical used to create nonstick surfaces. There is some concern that PFOA is transferred to food through cooking and, while the jury is still out, I think it pays to play it safe and use PFOA-free pans.

time to get started!

I think of cooking as a soulful activity. It gives you the opportunity to nourish both yourself and others not only with the nutrients we all need to thrive but also with the thoughtfulness and caring that so enrich our lives. I hope by helping you acquire a love of chia, these recipes allow you to throw more love out into the world. Enjoy!

juices, smoothies, and shakes

After the Aztecs were conquered by the Spanish, not a lot of chia traditions endured. But one that did was the chia drink. Agua fresca, a refreshing beverage served in Mexico, helped inspire Mamma Chia's beverages and also served as the inspiration for these chia juices, smoothies, and shakes (with one herbal infusion thrown in). Because the drinks all rely on chia gel as a base, they provide a great opportunity to learn about the different ways of making and flavoring the gel and seeing how beautifully it works to add body to a food. Once you've tried all the recipes in this chapter, go ahead and start using different chia gels to invent chia beverages of your own.

serrano pineapple-papaya smoothie

This smoothie is unusual for its heat, ably provided by both the serrano chile and the fresh ginger. The instructions call for room-temperature pineapple juice—that's the temperature best suited to creating chia gel—with chilled glasses to make the smoothie colder. If you like an even colder drink, pop the mixture into the freezer for 10 minutes before serving.

-------------------- SERVES 2 --------------------

1 cup 100% pure pineapple juice (not from concentrate), at room temperature

2 tablespoons white chia seeds

1 cup fresh papaya cubes

½ cup peeled, chopped English cucumber

½ small serrano pepper, with or without seeds, stemmed

1½ teaspoons freshly squeezed lime juice

1½ teaspoons pistachio or avocado oil

1 teaspoon peeled, grated fresh ginger

⅛ teaspoon sea salt

2 sprigs cilantro, for garnish

In a liquid measuring cup or small bowl, whisk together the pineapple juice and chia seeds and let stand for about 20 minutes. (Makes 1⅛ cups pineapple-chia gel.)

Place the pineapple-chia gel, papaya, cucumber, serrano pepper, lime juice, oil, ginger, and salt in a blender. Cover and puree until smooth.

Pour into two chilled martini or other beverage glasses. Garnish each with a cilantro sprig and serve.

cayenne-chia lemonade

Cayenne, maple syrup, and lemon is a classic cleanse recipe: both lemon and cayenne encourage the body to engage in its own natural cleaning process, releasing and flushing toxins and restoring balance (the maple syrup makes it all yummy). Adding fiber-rich chia to the mix just increases the lemonade's power to help you whisk toxins out of the body.

SERVES 1

1 tablespoon black or white chia seeds

1 cup plus 2 tablespoons purified water

1 tablespoon freshly squeezed lemon juice (from about ½ small lemon)

2 tablespoons pure maple syrup

Pinch of ground cayenne pepper

In a liquid measuring cup or small bowl, whisk together the chia seeds and the 2 tablespoons water and let stand for about 20 minutes. (Makes 3 tablespoons thick chia gel.)

In a large glass, briskly stir together the chia gel, the remaining 1 cup of water, lemon juice, maple syrup, and cayenne pepper. Add ice, if desired, and serve.

tarragon-mint cooler

This herbal infusion makes a nice change of pace from iced tea. Speckled with chia, it looks beautiful in a clear glass pitcher. If you prefer your "tea" unsweetened, simply leave out the honey or agave.

SERVES 4

3 tablespoons dried mint leaves

1 teaspoon dried tarragon

¼ cup black chia seeds

4 cups purified water

2 tablespoons agave nectar or honey

Mint sprigs, for garnish

Add the dried mint and tarragon to a metal tea infuser. Alternatively, wrap the herbs in a piece of cheesecloth and tie with kitchen twine or dental floss. Place the herbs in a heatproof container, such as a four-cup glass measuring cup, and add chia seeds.

Bring the water to a boil and pour over dried herbs and chia. Stir briskly to distribute chia and cover container with plastic wrap.

After 10 minutes, uncover and stir in the agave nectar. Allow the herbs to steep until the water cools. Remove infuser or cheesecloth from the container.

Pour into glasses filled with ice or chill in the refrigerator until cold. Stir before serving (the chia seeds will have floated to the top) and garnish each serving with a sprig of mint.

pomegranate, grapefruit, and ginger fizz

You could also call this bubbly drink "Antioxidant Blast." Chia is chock-full of the free-radical fighters quercetin, chlorogenic acid, caffeic acid, and kaempferol, while pomegranates are rich in punicalagin and anthocyanins. Add in the antioxidant powers of vitamin C from the grapefruit and lemon juices, and you've got a very tasty way to stay vibrant and healthy. When making this fizz, look for a ginger ale with fresh ginger. I like Fresh Ginger, Ginger Ale by Bruce Cost.

SERVES 2

¾ cup 100% pure pomegranate juice (not from concentrate), at room temperature

2 tablespoons white chia seeds

½ cup freshly squeezed pink grapefruit juice (from about ½ large pink grapefruit)

1 tablespoon freshly squeezed lemon juice (from about ½ small lemon)

6 fresh mint leaves

½ cup ginger ale

2 long, thin grapefruit peel spirals, for garnish

In a liquid measuring cup or small bowl, whisk together the pomegranate juice and chia seeds and let stand for about 20 minutes. (Makes ⅞ cup pomegranate-chia gel.)

Place the pomegranate-chia gel, grapefruit juice, lemon juice, and mint leaves in a blender. Cover and puree until smooth.

Pour into glasses filled with ice. Top with ginger ale. Garnish with grapefruit peel spirals and serve immediately.

mango lassi

Lassi is a rich-tasting Indian yogurt drink and a great match for spicy foods. It's versatile, too: If you prefer a savory beverage, add a pinch of cumin and salt. Opt for the cardamom and leave out the salt to add a bit of sweetness. Like all drink recipes, this one has a chia gel at its base. Using the gel ensures that the drink has an optimal consistency, not always the case when you just add chia seeds to already-blended ingredients.

-------------------------- SERVES 2 --------------------------

3 tablespoons black or white chia seeds

$1/2$ cup purified water or plain unsweetened almond milk

2 mangoes, peeled and pitted (about 1$1/2$ cups flesh)

1 cup plain yogurt

1 tablespoon agave nectar or honey

Pinch of ground cumin or cardamom

Pinch of sea salt (optional)

In a liquid measuring cup or small bowl, whisk together the chia seeds and water and let stand for about 20 minutes. (Makes about $2/3$ cup chia gel.)

Place the chia gel, mangoes, yogurt, agave nectar, cumin, and salt in a blender. Cover and blend on high until smooth.

Pour into glasses and serve.

chia green superfood smoothie

This superfood cleanse-style smoothie makes a supersatisfying snack. The apple juice and grapes give it just the right amount of sweetness, while the ginger and lemon provide a nice kick. If you add in a small handful of raw almonds and enjoy the whole recipe for yourself, you've got the perfect meal replacement.

SERVES 2

¾ cup 100% pure apple juice (not from concentrate), at room temperature

1 tablespoon white chia seeds

1 cup firmly packed fresh baby spinach or baby kale

1 cup seedless green grapes, frozen

½ cup chopped, peeled or unpeeled, English cucumber

¼ Hass avocado, peeled

¼ cup loosely packed fresh mint leaves

2 tablespoons freshly squeezed lemon juice (from about 1 small lemon)

2 teaspoons peeled, grated fresh ginger

In a liquid measuring cup or small bowl, whisk together the apple juice and chia seeds and let stand for about 20 minutes. (Makes about ⅞ cup apple-chia gel.)

Place the apple-chia gel, spinach, grapes, cucumber, avocado, mint, lemon juice, and ginger in a blender. Cover and puree until smooth. Pour into two glasses and serve immediately.

chia-berry shake

- -

As thick and smooth as a milk shake, this berry freeze actually gets its creaminess from chia and avocado, not milk and ice cream. Using frozen berries keeps the drink icy cold (and allows you to make it when berries are out of season), but if you prefer to use fresh, just add a couple of ice cubes when blending.

- SERVES 2 -

2 tablespoons black or white chia seeds

1 cup purified water

2 cups frozen mixed berries (such as blackberries, strawberries, blueberries, and marionberries), plus more for garnish (optional)

Pinch of ground cardamom

1 cup plain unsweetened almond milk

2 tablespoons agave nectar or honey

2 teaspoons pure vanilla extract

1/2 Hass avocado

In a liquid measuring cup or small bowl, whisk together the chia seeds and water and let stand for about 20 minutes. (Makes about 1 1/8 cups chia gel.)

Place the chia gel, frozen berries, cardamom, almond milk, agave nectar, vanilla, and avocado in a blender. Cover and blend on high until thick and creamy.

Pour into two glasses. Garnish with additional berries and serve immediately.

"bananas foster" chia smoothie

Bananas Foster, which originated in New Orleans, is perhaps one of the most decadent desserts around. Vanilla ice cream, loads of butter, cinnamon, brown sugar, rum . . . you get the idea. Here, you get those same lavish flavors without any of the guilt. Choose bananas that are just ripened, not fully or overripened, which can become too mushy during sautéing.

SERVES 2

1 cup plus 3 tablespoons unsweetened plain almond milk or coconut milk beverage

2 tablespoons black or white chia seeds

1 cup coconut or hemp milk–based vanilla frozen dessert or frozen yogurt

1 tablespoon plus 2 teaspoons honey or agave nectar

1/4 teaspoon pure almond extract

1 tablespoon unsalted butter

1/8 teaspoon ground cinnamon

Pinch of sea salt

1 medium just-ripened banana, sliced into 1/2-inch-thick coins

In a liquid measuring cup or small bowl, whisk together 1 cup of the almond milk and the chia seeds and let stand for about 20 minutes. (Makes 1 1/8 cups almond-chia gel.)

Place the almond-chia gel, frozen dessert, 2 teaspoons of the honey, and the almond extract in a blender. Cover and puree until smooth. Pour into two milk shake glasses or coffee mugs and place in the freezer.

While the smoothies are chilling in the freezer, melt the butter in a nonstick (PFOA-free) skillet over medium heat. Add the remaining 1 tablespoon of honey, cinnamon, and salt and stir until foamy, about 30 seconds. Briskly stir in the remaining 3 tablespoons of almond milk and bring to a full simmer, about 1 1/2 minutes. Add the banana coins and continue simmering until mixture becomes syrupy and banana coins are heated through, about 2 minutes.

Pour the hot banana mixture on top of each chilled smoothie, and enjoy with a spoon and straw.

chia, dark chocolate, and mint shake

Peppermint Patty fans, this one's for you! To make this minty chocolate shake, I use cacao powder, which is chocolate made from raw or lightly roasted beans. (Cocoa powder is made from more robustly roasted beans and can be substituted for cacao powder.) The low-temperature roasting preserves many of the nutrients inherent in the bean. As you shop for the cacao used to make this scrumptious shake, consider buying one that is fair-trade certified to assure that the farmers and workers are fairly compensated. That way, every shake you make will make both your taste buds and your spirit feel good.

SERVES 2

1 cup unsweetened plain coconut milk beverage, almond milk, or fat-free milk, at room temperature

2 tablespoons chia seeds

2 tablespoons unsweetened cacao powder or cocoa powder

1 cup vanilla frozen yogurt or coconut or hemp milk–based frozen dessert

1 teaspoon agave nectar or honey

1/8 teaspoon pure peppermint extract

Chill two tall glasses. In a liquid measuring cup or small bowl, stir together the coconut milk beverage and chia seeds and let stand for about 20 minutes. (Makes 1 1/8 cups coconut-chia gel.)

Place the coconut-chia gel, cacao powder, frozen yogurt, agave nectar, and peppermint extract in a blender. Cover and puree until smooth.

Pour into the chilled glasses and serve.

healthy mornings

Whether you like your breakfast savory or on the sweet side, you'll find a chia dish to accommodate your tastes. Likewise, there's variety in the complexity of these healthy morning meals. Some are quick and easy; they assemble in no time or can be made ahead so that you don't have to bother with cooking on days when you need to be out the door fast. Then there are dishes—some you may want to save for weekends—that are heartier and take a little longer to prepare. At my house, they pull double duty on "breakfast for dinner" nights!

chia-peach jam

When peaches are in season, they look so luscious that I often overbuy. Then I have to figure out what to do with all of them before they spoil. Here's the perfect solution: a summer treat that tastes wonderful on toasted whole grain bread. When you make jam with chia, you don't need to add pectin: the seeds supply all the gelling you need.

MAKES 1½ CUPS

5 fresh ripe peaches
5 tablespoons white chia seeds
2 tablespoons agave nectar
½ teaspoon ground cinnamon
1 teaspoon fresh lemon juice

Bring a pot of water to a boil. Have a large bowl filled with ice water ready next to the stove.

One at a time, place the peaches in the boiling water and scald for 30 seconds. Transfer immediately to the ice water to cool, and then peel off the skins.

Halve the peeled peaches, remove pits, and cut into chunks. Place in a food processor with the chia seeds, agave, cinnamon, and lemon juice. Puree until thick. Jam keeps for 1 week in the refrigerator, covered.

amazing chia banana nut muffins

- -

This is my kind of comfort food: moist, tender, cinnamony, and—thanks to both chia and walnuts (another good source of alpha-linolenic acid)—incredibly nutritious. It just so happens that these muffins are also free of gluten and dairy. A few notes on the ingredients: If you haven't cooked with coconut oil before, I think you'll be delighted to find that this rich, healthy fat makes a fantastic substitute for butter. In this recipe, make sure to use only gluten-free flour. If you replace it with regular flour, the muffins will come out rubbery. On a final note, if you hate wasting egg yolks, you can buy pre-separated whites, generally found in the refrigerated section of supermarkets.

- MAKES 12 MUFFINS -

¼ cup plus 2 tablespoons virgin coconut oil, plus more for greasing

1 tablespoon black or white chia seeds

3 tablespoons purified water

⅔ cup coarsely chopped walnuts

2 cups all-purpose gluten-free flour blend

½ teaspoon sea salt

½ teaspoon baking soda

½ teaspoon baking powder

½ teaspoon ground cinnamon

Preheat the oven to 350°F. Grease each cup of a nonstick (PFOA-free) muffin pan with coconut oil. Alternatively, line pan with 12 muffin cups.

In a small bowl, whisk together the chia seeds and water and let stand for about 20 minutes. (Makes ¼ cup chia gel.)

Place the walnuts on a sheet pan and toast in the oven for about 10 minutes, until fragrant. Transfer to a plate to cool.

Whisk together the flour, salt, baking soda, baking powder, and cinnamon in a large bowl.

In a separate bowl, combine the bananas, coconut oil, egg whites, chia gel, vanilla, and sugar with a wooden spoon. Add

3 medium bananas, coarsely mashed

Whites of 4 large eggs or ½ cup liquid 100% egg whites

1 teaspoon pure vanilla extract

1 cup coconut or date palm sugar

to dry ingredients and mix just until moistened. Fold in the walnuts. Using an ice cream scoop or spoon, divide batter among the muffin cups.

Bake until tops of muffins are lightly brown and a toothpick inserted into the center of a muffin comes out clean, about 25 minutes.

Remove the muffin pan from oven. Gently run a knife around each muffin and remove from the pan. Place muffins on a wire rack and cool completely. Serve warm or cool, or store well wrapped for later. Muffins keep well for 1 week at room temperature or 1 month in the freezer.

zucchini-chia muffins

If you like the moist, cinnamony taste of carrot cake, you're sure to like these muffins, which are spiked with a generous dose of chia. Make an extra dozen to freeze so you'll always have a delicious grab-and-go breakfast on hand.

MAKES 12

1 ¼ cups plus 3 tablespoons whole wheat pastry flour

¼ cup raw walnuts, chopped

¼ cup sliced raw almonds

⅓ cup milled (ground) chia seeds

½ teaspoon sea salt

¾ teaspoon baking powder

½ teaspoon baking soda

1 teaspoon ground cinnamon

2 large eggs

½ cup virgin coconut oil

¾ cup raw sugar

3 tablespoons no-sugar-added apple butter

1 ½ teaspoons pure vanilla extract

1 teaspoon grated lemon zest

1 cup coarsely grated unpeeled zucchini (do not drain excess liquid)

⅓ cup coarsely grated carrot

⅓ cup black seedless raisins or dried pineapple bits

Preheat the oven to 350°F. Coat each cup of a nonstick (PFOA-free) muffin pan with cooking spray and dust the cups with 3 tablespoons of the flour. Alternatively, line pan with 12 muffin cups.

Place the walnuts and almonds on a sheet pan and toast in the oven for about 10 minutes, until fragrant. Transfer to a plate to cool.

Whisk together the remaining 1¼ cups of flour, the chia, salt, baking powder, baking soda, and cinnamon in a bowl. In a separate large bowl, whisk together the eggs, oil, sugar, apple butter, vanilla, and lemon zest. Add the flour-chia mixture and whisk until just combined. Stir in the zucchini, carrot, raisins, walnuts, and almonds until evenly combined. Using an ice cream scoop or spoon, divide batter among the muffin cups.

Bake until a toothpick inserted into the center of a muffin comes out clean, about 22 minutes. Cool muffins in the pan on a rack. Serve warm or cool, or store well wrapped for later. Muffins keep well for 1 week at room temperature or 1 month in the freezer.

fajita-style chia breakfast wrap

Typically, you'd use eight eggs to make breakfast wraps for four people. Here, chia gel lets you cut the eggs in half, gaining fiber and omega-3s without losing any volume—it will still be as filling as an eight-egg dish. The size of your wraps will depend on which type of tortilla you use. Choose an 8-inch tortilla if you prefer a small wrap or large soft taco; opt for 10-inch if you'd like your wrap to be more like a burrito.

-------------------------- SERVES 4 --------------------------

1/4 cup black or white chia seeds

3/4 cup purified water

4 large eggs

1/2 teaspoon sea salt

1/4 teaspoon freshly ground black pepper

1/4 teaspoon adobo or Mexican seasoning (optional)

2 tablespoons extra-virgin olive oil

1 medium red bell pepper, thinly sliced

1 medium green bell pepper, thinly sliced

1 small or 1/2 large white onion, thinly sliced

1/2 cup shredded Monterey Jack or pepper Jack cheese

In a liquid measuring cup or small bowl, whisk together the chia seeds and water and let stand for about 20 minutes. (Makes 7/8 cup chia gel.)

In a large liquid measuring cup or bowl, whisk together the chia gel, eggs, 3/8 teaspoon of the salt, the pepper, and adobo seasoning. Set aside.

Meanwhile, heat 1 tablespoon of the oil in a nonstick (PFOA-free) skillet over medium-high heat. Add the bell peppers and sauté until just cooked through, about 4 minutes. Transfer to a serving dish. Place the skillet back on the stove over medium-high heat and heat the remaining 1 tablespoon of oil. Add the onion and the remaining 1/8 teaspoon of salt and sauté until softened and lightly caramelized, about 4 minutes. Add the egg mixture and cook while scrambling until eggs are no longer runny, 2 1/2 to 3 minutes. Stir in the cheese and cilantro, remove from heat, taste, and adjust seasonings. Transfer to a separate serving dish.

2 tablespoons chopped fresh cilantro

½ Hass avocado, pitted, peeled, and sliced

4 (8- to 10-inch) whole grain or chia seed tortillas, warmed

1 lime, cut into wedges

½ cup Fresh Cherry Tomato–Green Onion Salsa (page 72) or pico de gallo, drained of excess liquid

Place the avocado, tortillas, and limes on separate plates and spoon the salsa into a bowl. Serve everything family-style and allow guests to make their own wraps.

sticky brown rice with sunny-side-up egg

This dish was inspired by *tamago kake gohan*, a popular Japanese breakfast food. It's best made with leftover rice (freshly made rice tends to become too mushy). If you don't have any on hand, make the rice the night before.

SERVES 2

1/2 cup low-sodium vegetable broth

1 green onion, sliced on diagonal, green and white parts separated

2 tablespoons plus 1/2 teaspoon black or white chia seeds

2 cups cooked, chilled short-grain brown rice

1 1/2 teaspoons toasted sesame oil

2 large eggs

1 tablespoon tamari soy sauce

In a small saucepan, stir together the broth, white parts of green onion, and 2 tablespoons of the chia seeds and let stand for about 20 minutes. (Makes about 2/3 cup green onion–chia gel.)

Bring the green onion–chia gel to a boil over high heat. Add the rice and stir for about 30 seconds. Cover, reduce heat to low, and cook until rice is steaming hot and has a sticky consistency, about 4 minutes.

Meanwhile, heat the oil in a nonstick (PFOA-free) skillet over medium heat. Add the eggs and cook until desired doneness, such as sunny-side up, about 4 minutes.

Divide the sticky rice mixture onto plates or into bowls and top each with an egg. Sprinkle with the tamari, the remaining 1/2 teaspoon of chia seeds, and the green parts of green onion. Serve immediately.

overnight caprese baked egg

- -

Caprese, the beloved combo of fresh mozzarella, tomato, and basil, needn't be relegated to afternoons and evenings. Here it's served up for breakfast over chia bread pudding with a simple preparation technique: assemble it in the evening, and then simply pop it into the oven in the morning.

- SERVES 1 -

1 large egg

2 tablespoons purified water

1 tablespoon half-and-half

1 tablespoon white chia seeds

1/4 teaspoon plus a pinch of sea salt

Pinch of red pepper flakes

1 (3/4-ounce) slice Italian or French baguette, about 1/2 inch thick, cut into small cubes

1 (1-ounce) slice fresh lightly salted mozzarella cheese, or 1/4 cup shredded mozzarella cheese

1 (1/4-inch-thick) slice medium vine-ripened tomato

1/2 teaspoon extra-virgin olive oil

1 sprig basil

Coat a 6-ounce ramekin with olive oil cooking spray.

In a liquid measuring cup or small bowl, whisk together the egg, water, half-and-half, chia seeds, 1/4 teaspoon of the salt, and the red pepper flakes and let stand for about 20 minutes.

Pack the baguette cubes into the ramekin. Whisk the egg mixture again and pour over baguette cubes. Let stand for 5 minutes to allow bread to absorb egg mixture. Top with the cheese, tomato, and the remaining pinch of salt. Cover ramekin and chill overnight.

Preheat oven to 350°F. Place chilled ramekin on a small baking sheet and bake until egg mixture is fully cooked and cheese is melted, about 22 minutes. Drizzle with the olive oil, garnish with basil, and serve.

hot madras tofu-chia scramble with greens

If you like your breakfast savory, this curry scramble will fill the bill. It's also a great dinner dish. Take a few seconds to make the chia gel in the morning, and you can have dinner on the table in fifteen minutes.

SERVES 4

4 tablespoons black or white chia seeds

1 cup purified water

2 teaspoons fresh lemon juice

14 ounces extra-firm tofu, drained and cut into 1/2-inch cubes

1 1/4 teaspoons sea salt

3/4 teaspoon hot Madras curry powder

1/2 teaspoon ground coriander or ground cumin

1/4 teaspoon freshly ground black pepper

2 1/2 tablespoons virgin coconut oil

1 medium white onion, finely diced

5 cups firmly packed fresh baby spinach, or a mixture of baby spinach and finely chopped mustard greens (about 5 ounces)

1 medium vine-ripened tomato, pulp removed and finely diced

2 tablespoons chopped fresh cilantro

In a liquid measuring cup or small bowl, whisk together 3 tablespoons of the chia seeds, water, and lemon juice and let stand for about 20 minutes. (Makes about 1 1/3 cups lemon-chia gel.)

Meanwhile, place the tofu, 3/4 teaspoon of the salt, the curry powder, coriander, and black pepper in a bowl. Stir well to combine and set aside.

Heat the oil in a large nonstick (PFOA-free) skillet over medium-high heat. Add the onion and sauté until softened, about 5 minutes. Add the tofu mixture and sauté until onions are fully softened and tofu resembles scrambled eggs, about 8 minutes. Add the spinach, lemon-chia gel, and the remaining 1/2 teaspoon of salt and cook while stirring until the spinach is wilted, about 1 minute. Add the tomato and cilantro and cook while stirring until tomato is heated through, about 1 minute. Taste and adjust seasonings.

Transfer to individual bowls, sprinkle with the remaining 1 tablespoon of chia seeds, and serve.

roasted turkey, thyme, and chia breakfast sausage patties

Making sausage yourself is a lot easier than you might think, and these chia-spiked patties have the advantage of being lighter and less greasy than traditional sausage. They're very flavorful as is, but if you want to give them even more of a punch, mix the chia seeds with 1/2 cup low-sodium vegetable or chicken broth instead of the purified water. You can also use this recipe to create meatballs—just form mixture into 24 balls instead of 12 and skip the step where you flatten the sausage into patties.

SERVES 4

1/4 cup black or white chia seeds

1/2 cup purified water

1 pound ground turkey (about 93% lean)

3/4 cup rolled (old-fashioned) oats

1/3 cup coarsely grated or minced red onion

1/4 cup unsweetened applesauce or apple-peach sauce

3 tablespoons finely chopped fresh flat-leaf parsley

1 1/2 tablespoons extra-virgin olive oil

2 teaspoons ground sage

1 1/2 teaspoons finely chopped fresh thyme leaves

2 teaspoons Dijon mustard

1 teaspoon sea salt

1 teaspoon fennel seeds

3/4 teaspoon red pepper flakes

3/4 teaspoon freshly ground black pepper

Preheat the oven to 475°F.

In a liquid measuring cup or small bowl, whisk together the chia seeds and water and let stand for about 20 minutes. (Makes 3/4 cup extra-thick chia gel.)

In a large bowl, use your hands to evenly combine the chia gel, ground turkey, oats, onion, applesauce, parsley, oil, sage, thyme, mustard, salt, fennel seeds, red pepper flakes, and black pepper.

Line a large rimmed baking sheet with aluminum foil and coat with cooking spray. Form mixture into 12 balls, 1/4 rounded cup each, and place on baking sheet. Press down on each to form about 3 1/2-inch-diameter patties. Place in oven and roast until well done, about 17 minutes.

Remove from oven, let stand 5 minutes to complete the cooking process, and serve warm.

chia and herb–sweet potato hash browns

As far as I'm concerned, all hash browns are good hash browns—yum!
But these hash browns also happen to be *good-for-you* hash browns. With
the combination of chia (which adds to their delicate crunch) and sweet
potatoes, they deliver plenty of antioxidants. Serve with a side of eggs or
scrambled tofu.

SERVES 4

¼ cup extra-virgin olive oil

1¼ pounds sweet potatoes
(about 3 medium), unpeeled,
scrubbed, ends trimmed, cut
into ½-inch cubes

1 medium yellow or white
onion, diced

2 teaspoons apple cider vinegar

1 teaspoon sea salt

⅛ teaspoon ground cayenne
pepper

3 tablespoons chopped fresh
flat-leaf parsley

1 tablespoon chopped fresh
tarragon

2 tablespoons black chia seeds

Heat the oil in a large nonstick(PFOA-free) skillet over
medium-high heat. Add the potatoes, onion, vinegar, ¼ teaspoon of the salt, and cayenne. Stir to combine. Cover and
cook until the onion is softened, about 8 minutes, stirring once
halfway through the cooking.

Remove lid and sauté until the sweet potatoes are cooked
through and lightly browned, about 8 minutes. Add the
parsley, tarragon, and the remaining ¾ teaspoon of salt and
sauté for 1 minute. Taste and adjust seasonings.

Transfer to a serving dish, sprinkle with or stir in chia seeds,
and serve immediately.

cinnamon apple orchard hotcakes

Milled chia and whole wheat pastry flour fill in for all-purpose flour in these nontraditional hotcakes, upping their fiber and protein content considerably. Be sure to slice the apple very thin so that it "melts" into the hotcakes.

SERVES 4

CINNAMON MAPLE SYRUP
1/2 cup pure maple syrup
1/4 teaspoon ground cinnamon

1 1/2 cups whole wheat pastry flour
1/4 cup milled (ground) chia seeds
2 teaspoons baking powder
1/4 teaspoon sea salt
1/2 teaspoon cinnamon
2 large eggs
1 3/4 cups plain unsweetened almond milk or coconut milk beverage
2 tablespoons honey or agave nectar
1 teaspoon pure vanilla extract
1 large Granny Smith apple, cored, halved, and thinly sliced

Preheat the oven to 200°F.

To make the syrup, in a small saucepan, stir together the maple syrup and cinnamon and warm over low heat. Cover and set aside.

Whisk together the flour, chia, baking powder, salt, and cinnamon in a large bowl. In another bowl, whisk together the eggs, almond milk, honey, and vanilla. Slowly add liquid mixture to the dry mixture and whisk until combined. Set aside for 10 minutes.

Meanwhile, wrap the apple slices well in unbleached parchment paper, place on a microwave-safe plate, and cook in the microwave on high for 2 minutes, or until softened. Or wrap the apple slices well in aluminum foil and bake in a preheated 400°F oven until softened, 20 to 25 minutes. Unwrap and set aside.

Coat a large nonstick (PFOA-free) skillet or griddle with cooking spray and heat over medium heat. Ladle about 1/3 cup of the batter onto the hot skillet, tilting to form a 6-inch-diameter hotcake. (You should have enough to make 8 pancakes.) Arrange 1/8 of the apple slices on top. Cook until hotcake is browned on both sides, about 3 minutes per side. Keep warm on a baking sheet in the oven while preparing the remaining hotcakes. Serve drizzled with the warm syrup.

peach melba amaranth porridge

Amaranth and chia are a natural pair—both were beloved by the Aztecs. Here they get the "melba" treatment: mixed with peaches and topped with a dessertlike raspberry sauce for a sumptuous yet healthy breakfast.

SERVES 4

2 large ripe peaches

3/4 cup fresh or frozen raspberries, thawed

2 teaspoons agave nectar or honey

2 teaspoons fresh lemon juice

1 cup whole grain amaranth

1/4 cup black or white chia seeds

2 cups coconut milk beverage or almond milk

1 2/3 cups purified water

1 teaspoon pure vanilla extract

1/4 teaspoon sea salt

1/4 cup vanilla Greek or Icelandic yogurt or frozen yogurt

Bring a pot of water to a boil. Have a large bowl filled with ice water ready next to the stove.

One at a time, place the peaches in the boiling water and scald for 30 seconds. Transfer immediately to the ice water to cool, and then peel off the skins.

Halve the peaches, remove pits, and dice. Set aside.

To make the raspberry syrup, place the raspberries, agave nectar, and lemon juice in a blender. Cover and puree. Set aside (leaving raspberry seeds in the puree).

To make the porridge, place the amaranth, chia seeds, coconut milk beverage, water, vanilla, salt, and reserved peaches in a large saucepan and stir to combine. Bring to a boil over high heat. Reduce heat to medium-low and simmer uncovered, stirring frequently, until amaranth is tender and desired consistency is reached, about 25 minutes.

Transfer the hot cereal to four individual bowls, top with yogurt and raspberry syrup, and serve.

blueberry compote parfaits

- -

I think of yogurt like a blank canvas: it provides a wonderful base for any art-
ful combination of flavors you add to it. In this case, it's a lovely mix of chia and
blueberries in syrup layered with granola for added crunch. This recipe will
also work well with any other fruit you have on hand.

- SERVES 4 -

BLUEBERRY COMPOTE

2 cups fresh or frozen
blueberries

¾ cup purified water

⅓ cup coconut or date palm
sugar

¼ cup black or white chia seeds

1 teaspoon fresh lemon juice

2 cups granola cereal

2 cups plain Greek or Icelandic
yogurt

1 teaspoon black or white
chia seeds

To make the compote, place the blueberries, water, sugar,
and chia seeds in a saucepan and bring to a boil. Lower to a
simmer and cook until slightly thickened, 8 to 10 minutes. Stir
in the lemon juice. Set aside and allow to cool.

To prepare the parfaits, divide the three main ingredients
among four parfait glasses or bowls, beginning with a layer
of granola, then the Greek yogurt, and finally the blueberry
compote. Sprinkle ¼ teaspoon chia seeds over each parfait
and serve.

chia, white chocolate, and macadamia granola bars

- -

Eating breakfast on the run sounds inherently unhealthy, but it doesn't have to be. These granola bars, the perfect grab-and-go morning meal, are packed with protein, fiber, and omega-3s—though they taste as decadent as a donut. If you like, you can make them gluten-free by swapping flours. Just remember to use gluten-free oats, too.

- MAKES 15 BARS -

$\frac{1}{3}$ cup plus 2 teaspoons virgin coconut oil

2 $\frac{1}{4}$ cups rolled (old-fashioned) oats

1 cup whole wheat pastry flour or all-purpose gluten-free flour

$\frac{3}{4}$ cup raw sugar

$\frac{1}{2}$ cup milled (ground) chia seeds

$\frac{1}{2}$ teaspoon ground cinnamon

$\frac{1}{3}$ cup chopped lightly salted or unsalted macadamia nuts

$\frac{1}{3}$ cup high-quality white chocolate chips

1 teaspoon sea salt

$\frac{1}{3}$ cup honey or agave nectar

$\frac{1}{3}$ cup creamy natural peanut or almond butter

2 large eggs

1 $\frac{1}{2}$ teaspoons pure vanilla extract

$\frac{1}{2}$ teaspoon pure almond extract

Preheat the oven to 350°F. Grease a nonstick (PFOA-free) 9 by 13-inch baking pan with 2 teaspoons of the coconut oil. Set aside.

In a large bowl, stir together the oats, flour, sugar, chia, cinnamon, nuts, white chocolate chips, and salt.

In another bowl, stir together the honey, nut butter, and the remaining $\frac{1}{3}$ cup of coconut oil. Add the eggs and vanilla and almond extracts and vigorously stir with a fork.

Add the honey mixture to the oat mixture and stir with a silicone spoon or spatula until evenly combined. Transfer to the prepared baking pan, pressing down on the mixture to fill the pan evenly and compactly. Bake until edges begin to brown, about 30 minutes.

Let stand for 10 minutes to cool slightly, then cut into 15 bars in the pan. Place pan on a wire rack and cool completely. Remove the bars from the pan and serve. Store individually wrapped in unbleached parchment paper, then aluminum foil, at room temperature for up to 3 days, or freeze for up to 3 months.

snacks and small bites

In this chapter, you'll find both new ideas for nibbles and a few classics given healthy makeovers. Chia works especially well to give snacks more crunch (you won't miss the frying usually associated with crunchy snacks), and it's a terrific way to help dips hold together, reducing the need for large amounts of traditional thickeners like cream cheese. I find that small bites are a particularly good way to introduce newbies to chia. Tote along a jar of Honey-Sesame Chia Snack Mix (page 62) or Chia Spiced California Walnuts (page 64) as a hostess gift when you're invited to a friend's home for dinner, or serve one of the chia dips when you're the one having guests—either way, they'll be hooked!

honey-sesame chia snack mix

If you like caramel corn, you'll delight in this sweet, salty, and slightly spicy souped-up version with chia seeds, sesame seeds, and cashews. Look for non-GMO or organic popcorn in your supermarket—corn is one of the most prevalent GMO crops.

MAKES ABOUT 6 CUPS

$1/3$ cup mild honey or agave nectar

1 tablespoon virgin coconut oil

$1/2$ teaspoon plus $1/8$ teaspoon sea salt

$1/4$ teaspoon ground cayenne pepper

6 cups popped popcorn

$3/4$ cup raw cashews

$1/4$ cup black or white chia seeds

1 tablespoon white sesame seeds

Preheat the oven to 325°F. Lightly coat a large rimmed baking sheet or two 9 by 13-inch baking pans with cooking spray.

In a small bowl, whisk together the honey, oil, $1/2$ teaspoon of the salt, and cayenne.

In a large bowl, stir together the popped popcorn and cashews. Drizzle with the honey mixture and stir until well coated. Sprinkle with the chia and sesame seeds and stir to evenly coat.

Arrange the popcorn mixture in a single layer on the prepared baking sheet. Bake until the cashews are caramelized, about 15 minutes, stirring once during baking. Remove from the oven, sprinkle with the remaining $1/8$ teaspoon of salt, and cool on a wire rack (the popcorn will crisp up as it cools). Serve at room temperature as a snack. The mix will keep in an airtight container at room temperature for up to 10 days.

chia spiced california walnuts

Like chia, walnuts are another great source of plant-based omega-3s and have been shown to reduce both total cholesterol and LDL (bad) cholesterol. These spicy-sweet, chia-coated nuts are delicious as a snack or sprinkled onto salads.

SERVES 4

2 tablespoons agave nectar or honey

1 teaspoon walnut oil or extra-virgin olive oil

1 cup raw walnut halves

1/4 cup milled (ground) chia seeds

1/2 teaspoon ground cayenne pepper

1/4 teaspoon ground cinnamon

1/4 teaspoon sea salt

Preheat the oven to 300°F. Line a baking sheet with unbleached parchment paper.

Whisk together the agave nectar and oil in a bowl. Add the walnuts and stir to fully coat.

In a small bowl, stir together the chia, cayenne, cinnamon, and salt. Sprinkle over the walnuts and gently stir to evenly coat.

Spread the walnut mixture in a single layer on the prepared baking sheet. Bake until toasted through, about 25 minutes. Cool on a wire rack (the walnut coating will crisp as they cool) and then serve. Store in an airtight container for up to a week, or freeze for later use.

truffle cauliflower "popcorn" with chia seeds

We have the good fortune to be living in a time when you can find all kinds of wonderful salts on the market. One of my favorites is truffle salt, which provides an easy way to add the earthy taste of those prized mushrooms without the high cost. Here it teams with chia to enhance cauliflower that's been cut into bite-size pieces and roasted to evoke popcorn. Makes a nice side dish as well as a snack.

SERVES 4

¼ cup black or white chia seeds

½ teaspoon truffle salt

1 medium head cauliflower, cut into small bite-size florets (about 8 cups)

3 tablespoons extra-virgin olive oil

Preheat the oven to 475°F.

In a small bowl, stir together the chia seeds and truffle salt. Set aside.

Place the cauliflower in a large bowl. Drizzle with the olive oil and toss to coat. Transfer the cauliflower to a large rimmed baking sheet and arrange in a single layer. Roast, stirring occasionally, until tender and caramelized, about 30 minutes.

Transfer the cauliflower to a large bowl, sprinkle with the chia-truffle salt mixture, and toss to coat. Taste and adjust seasonings. Serve immediately.

gluten-free sun-dried tomato chia crackers

Store-bought crackers are fine. But homemade crackers? A step above. While this recipe, which combines the nutritional power of both chia and hemp seeds, does take a little effort to create, the result is amazing: a healthy, crispy cracker perfect for pairing with all kinds of spreads and dips—or just nibbling on its own. In fact, you can double the recipe if you like and bake in batches to make a party-ready 4 dozen crackers.

MAKES ABOUT 2 DOZEN CRACKERS

1 cup purified water

¼ cup packed sun-dried tomatoes (not packed in oil)

1 teaspoon chopped fresh rosemary

½ cup raw whole natural almonds

¼ cup steel-cut oats

¼ cup black chia seeds

1 tablespoon extra-virgin olive oil

1 teaspoon sea salt

⅛ teaspoon garlic powder

¼ cup milled (ground) chia seeds

¼ cup hemp seeds

Preheat the oven to 300°F. Cover the back of two large baking sheets each with a piece of unbleached parchment paper, wrapping the ends under the baking sheets to secure. Place pans on towels instead of directly on counter to allow for more traction when rolling out the cracker mixture.

In a small saucepan, bring water to a boil. Add the sun-dried tomatoes and rosemary, cover, remove from heat, and allow to sit for 10 minutes, until tomatoes have fully rehydrated. Do not drain.

Meanwhile, place the almonds, oats, chia seeds, oil, salt, and garlic powder in a food processor, cover, and blend until finely crumbled, about 1 minute. Add the hot water-tomato mixture, cover, and blend until well combined, about 1 minute.

Transfer to a medium mixing bowl, add the milled chia and hemp seeds, and stir to fully combine. Set aside for 10 minutes to allow all ingredients to fully hydrate and stir again to assure that everything is evenly combined.

Place half of the cracker mixture on top of each prepared baking sheet and cover each with a piece of parchment paper the same size as the baking sheet. Press down by hand to form a slightly flattened disk. Then use a rolling pin to thinly roll out each to about a 10 by 12-inch rectangle. Very gently peel off the parchment paper and discard. If desired, trim off excess parchment paper used for wrapping around the pan edges.

Bake both baking sheets until crackers are firm, yet not crisp, about 45 minutes. Remove from the oven and carefully cut into rectangles, about 12 per pan. Return to oven and continue to bake until nearly crisp, about 10 minutes more. Peel the crackers off of the parchment paper and place crackers directly onto the baking sheets. Turn oven off and let crackers crisp up in the oven as they cool, about 45 minutes. Remove crackers from the baking sheets and cool completely on a wire rack. Enjoy immediately for best results. To recrisp after storage in an airtight container, place in a 200°F oven for about 40 minutes.

tarragon-mustard kale chips

Way better for you than potato chips, these kale chips are a little bit salty, deliciously savory, and extra crispy thanks to both ground and whole chia. If you're not familiar with nutritional yeast, it's a dried product that has an almost cheeselike flavor and tons of B vitamins. You can find it in co-ops and natural foods stores. You can make the chips with any kind of kale, but the curly variety holds the seasonings best.

SERVES 6

One bunch curly kale (about 9 ounces)

1/8 cup milled (ground) chia seeds

1 1/2 teaspoons Dijon mustard

1/2 cup purified water

1/4 cup nutritional yeast

3/4 teaspoon sea salt

1 teaspoon dried tarragon

1 teaspoon fresh lemon juice

1 1/2 tablespoons extra-virgin olive oil

1 tablespoon chia seeds

Preheat the oven to 275°F. Line a baking sheet with unbleached parchment paper or aluminum foil.

Wash the kale and pat dry. Running your fingers down the spine of each leaf, pull the rib loose from the leaf. Discard the ribs. It's okay if the leaves tear, though they will be easier to handle if you leave them as whole as possible. Set aside.

In a shallow bowl, whisk together the milled chia, mustard, water, nutritional yeast, salt, tarragon, lemon juice, and oil until smooth. Add the kale leaves and toss to coat. (Using tongs helps ensure the mixture is distributed evenly.) Spread the leaves out on the prepared baking sheet. If the baking sheet is too crowded (the leaves are lying on top of each other), use two pans. This helps ensure that the kale gets crispy. Sprinkle leaves evenly with the whole chia seeds. Bake until the kale is pale green and crisp, about 1 to 1 1/2 hours, turning leaves once about halfway through.

Remove the kale-covered parchment from the baking sheet and place on a wire rack. Allow chips to cool. Store in an airtight container for up to 3 days.

yellow squash and zucchini flapjacks

These flapjacks are a fresh alternative to potato pancakes, especially in the summer when the farmers' market tables are overflowing with yellow squash and zucchini. They're perfect as an appetizer or a side dish. For a topping, use either sour cream or quark, a yogurtlike cheese that's lower in calories and higher in protein.

SERVES 4

1 medium yellow summer squash (about 8 ounces)

1 medium zucchini (about 8 ounces)

¾ teaspoon sea salt

⅓ cup whole wheat pastry flour or all-purpose gluten-free flour

¼ cup milled (ground) chia seeds

¼ teaspoon baking powder

⅛ teaspoon ground cayenne pepper

1 large egg, lightly beaten

1 green onion, green and white parts, minced

2 teaspoons chopped fresh dill or chives, plus more for garnish (optional)

½ cup extra-virgin olive oil, for frying

⅓ cup sour cream or quark

Coarsely grate the yellow squash and zucchini. Do not drain or squeeze off excess liquids. Transfer the squash and any liquids created during grating to a bowl. Toss with the salt and set aside.

Whisk together the flour, chia, baking powder, and cayenne in a large bowl. Add the squash mixture, egg, green onion, and dill. Stir until evenly combined.

Heat the oil in a nonstick (PFOA-free) skillet over medium heat. In 3 batches of 4 flapjacks each, place 2 heaping tablespoons of the batter per flapjack in the hot oil and flatten with the back of a spatula. Fry until well caramelized, about 4 to 4½ minutes per side. Drain on unbleached paper towels. Repeat with the remaining flapjack batter.

Serve topped with the sour cream and garnished with fresh dill.

plantain chips with avocado-chia dip

Plantain chips are a nice change of pace from tortilla chips as an accompaniment for this dip—and this dip doesn't have to be used as a dip at all: it also makes a delicious spread for sandwiches and burgers, and a tasty "bed" for grilled fish, too. Plus, you'll have plenty of dip left over—the recipe here makes 1¹/₂ cups, about double what you'll need to accompany the plantain chips.

SERVES 4 TO 6

AVOCADO-CHIA DIP

¹/₄ cup white chia seeds

1 tablespoon freshly squeezed lime juice (from about ¹/₂ lime)

¹/₂ cup purified water

1 Hass avocado, pitted and peeled

2 tablespoons classic mayonnaise or vegan mayonnaise

2 tablespoons plain Greek or Icelandic yogurt

1 clove garlic, peeled and minced

¹/₂ teaspoon sea salt

¹/₈ teaspoon ground cayenne pepper

3 large green (unripened) plantains, at room temperature

¹/₄ cup extra-virgin olive oil

¹/₂ teaspoon sea salt

1 lime, cut into wedges

To make the dip, in a mixing bowl, whisk together the chia seeds, lime juice, and water and let stand for about 20 minutes. (Makes ³/₄ cup chia gel.)

Add the avocado, mayonnaise, yogurt, garlic, salt, and cayenne to the chia mixture and mix with an electric mixer until fluffy. Adjust seasonings, and chill until ready to serve.

Preheat the oven to 375°F.

Cut off ends of the plantains. Cut 4 lengthwise slits into the skin of each (not into the fruit) and then peel. Thinly slice on the diagonal, about ¹/₈ inch thick.

Toss together plantains, oil, and salt in a bowl. Arrange plantains in a single layer on two large baking sheets. Bake until caramelized and crisp, 28 to 30 minutes.

Drain the plantains on unbleached paper towels and transfer to a platter. Serve with the dip and lime wedges. You can refrigerate any leftover dip in an airtight container for up to 3 days.

fresh cherry tomato–green onion salsa

Nothing is nicer on a hot day than throwing a few perfect ingredients into the food processor and coming out with a bright, spicy salsa in less than a minute. The recipe also calls for one chile pepper, but feel free to add more if you like your salsa tongue-scalding hot. Use the salsa on tacos or serve it with chips. My personal preference is to serve it with thick wedges of jicama sprinkled with salt and lime or spooned over grilled fish.

MAKES 1½ CUPS

1 pint cherry tomatoes

1 serrano or small jalapeño pepper, stemmed

2 tablespoons black or white chia seeds

5 green onions, white and green parts, coarsely chopped

2 tablespoons freshly squeezed lime juice (from about 1 lime)

1½ teaspoons sea salt

½ teaspoon ground cumin (optional)

Place all ingredients in a food processor. Cover and pulse until coarsely chopped. Let stand for at least 20 minutes to allow flavors to blend and chia to hydrate. Serve immediately, or cover and store in the refrigerator for up to 3 days.

smoky baba ghanoush

I have always loved Middle Eastern flavors and spices. On a trip to Turkey, I had some of the best food of my life—and one of my favorite dishes is the smoky, rich eggplant spread called baba ghanoush. While many store-bought versions lack flavor, homemade baba ghanoush is absolutely scrumptious. The key Is to really blacken the eggplant until the flesh is meltingly soft and has a smoky flavor. You can do it on a hot grill or over the gas burner on your stove. The dip is usually served with flat bread, but I also love it with crisp vegetables like cucumber.

SERVES 6

One large (or two small) Italian (globe) eggplant

1 tablespoon white chia seeds

3 tablespoons purified water

¼ cup tahini

1½ tablespoons freshly squeezed lemon juice (from about ½ lemon)

1 large clove garlic, peeled and minced

3 tablespoons extra-virgin olive oil

1 tablespoon chopped fresh flat-leaf parsley

1 tablespoon chopped fresh cilantro

Pinch of ground cumin

Sea salt

Puncture the eggplant in a few places with the tip of a knife. Roast on a hot grill over direct high heat, turning frequently, until charred and collapsed. Alternatively, spear the eggplant through the stem end with a carving fork. Turn a gas flame on your stove to high and place the eggplant directly on the burner, turning frequently with the fork, until the skin is charred and the flesh is soft, about 15 minutes. Wrap in aluminum foil and set aside to steam for about 20 minutes.

In a small bowl, whisk together the chia seeds and water and let stand for about 20 minutes. (Makes ¼ cup thick chia gel.)

Stir together the chia gel, tahini, lemon juice, garlic, oil, parsley, cilantro, cumin, and a pinch of salt in a large bowl. When the eggplant is ready, discard any accumulated juices and rub off blackened skin. Scoop the flesh into the bowl with the other ingredients. Stir vigorously to combine and break up the eggplant until silky and free of lumps. Adjust seasonings and lemon juice, if necessary. Serve immediately, or cover and store in the refrigerator for up to 3 days.

snacks and small bites

eggplant "caviar"

This eggplant dip has a tangier flavor than the Smoky Baba Ghanoush (page 73), and a more saladlike texture thanks to tomato, green onions, and chopped mint. Serve with whole grain crackers.

(page 73)

----- MAKES ABOUT 4 CUPS -----

2 tablespoons black or white chia seeds

¼ cup plus 1 tablespoon purified water

2 tablespoons balsamic vinegar

1 teaspoon naturally brewed soy sauce or coconut aminos

1 large globe eggplant

1 large tomato, diced, juices reserved

½ cup pine nuts

½ cup currants

1 green onion, green and white parts, minced

2 cloves garlic, peeled and minced

1 tablespoon chopped fresh mint

2 tablespoons extra-virgin olive oil

1 tablespoon freshly squeezed lemon juice (from about ½ small lemon)

1 teaspoon sea salt

In a liquid measuring cup or small bowl, stir together the chia seeds, water, vinegar, and soy sauce and let stand for about 20 minutes. (Makes about ³⁄₄ cups soy-chia gel.)

Puncture the eggplant in a few places with the tip of a knife. Roast on a hot grill over direct high heat, turning frequently, until charred and collapsed. Alternatively, spear the eggplant through the stem end with a carving fork. Turn a gas flame on your stove to high and place the eggplant directly on the burner, turning frequently with the fork, until the skin is charred and the flesh is soft, about 15 minutes. Wrap in aluminum foil and set aside to steam, about 20 minutes. When cool, scoop out flesh from skins and place in a large bowl.

Mash the eggplant flesh with a fork. Add the soy-chia gel, tomato with reserved juices, pine nuts, currants, green onion, garlic, mint, oil, lemon juice, and salt and stir well. Taste and adjust seasonings.

Cover and refrigerate for at least 2 hours to allow flavors to blend before serving. Leftovers can be stored, covered, in the refrigerator for up to 3 days.

cumin, chia seed, and cucumber raita

Raita is an Indian dish used as a dip or sauce. Its cooling yogurt base is a nice foil to curries and other spicy foods. Most Indian restaurants serve one type of raita, but as I learned from traveling in India, there are many, many variations on the theme. I like this one for its simplicity and, because of the added chia, its modernity. Pair with whole grain naan or Indian curry dishes.

MAKES 3 CUPS

½ large English cucumber, unpeeled (about 8 ounces)

1½ cups plain yogurt (not Greek yogurt)

⅓ cup plus 2 teaspoons chia seeds (preferably ⅓ cup white; 2 teaspoons black)

1½ teaspoons brown rice vinegar

1 green onion, green and white parts, minced

2 tablespoons finely chopped fresh cilantro

2 tablespoons finely chopped fresh mint

¾ teaspoon sea salt

½ teaspoon ground cumin

Coarsely grate the cucumber and transfer to a bowl along with all cucumber liquids. Stir in the yogurt, ⅓ cup of the chia seeds, and the vinegar and let stand for about 20 minutes.

Add the green onion, cilantro, mint, salt, and cumin to the chia-cucumber mixture and stir until well combined. Chill until ready to serve.

Taste and adjust seasonings. Sprinkle with the remaining 2 teaspoons of chia seeds and serve. Or cover and store in the refrigerator for up to 3 days.

chia hummus with sun-dried tomatoes and za'atar

Za'atar is a Middle Eastern mixture of herbs, sesame, and salt that gives food a nice, well, herbaceous, sesame, and salty flavor. Once only available in Middle Eastern grocery stores, it's increasingly available in supermarkets. If you can't find it, use thyme to give this hummus a kick. Serve hummus with an array of vegetable dippers, including carrots and cucumbers. You can add a handful of pita chips or Gluten-Free Sun-Dried Tomato Chia Crackers (page 66) for the carb-cravers in your crowd, too.

MAKES 2¾ CUPS

¼ cup white chia seeds

¾ cup plus ¼ cup purified water

3 tablespoons freshly squeezed lemon juice (from about 1 lemon)

8 sun-dried tomatoes (not oil packed)

1 (15-ounce) can chickpeas, drained

¼ cup tahini

1½ teaspoons dried za'atar or chopped fresh thyme leaves

2 large cloves garlic, peeled and chopped

½ teaspoon sea salt

1 tablespoon extra-virgin olive oil

In a liquid measuring cup or small bowl, whisk together the chia seeds, ¾ cup water, and the lemon juice and let stand for about 20 minutes. (Makes 1⅛ cups lemon-chia gel.)

Bring ¼ cup water to a simmer. Place the sun-dried tomatoes in a coffee mug or small heatproof bowl and add the water. Let stand for about 20 minutes.

Place the lemon-chia gel, sun-dried tomatoes with water, chickpeas, tahini, za'atar, garlic, and salt in a food processor or blender. Cover and puree. Taste and adjust seasonings. Chill until ready to serve.

To serve, spoon into a serving bowl and drizzle with olive oil. Or cover and store in the refrigerator for up to 1 week.

baked shiitake, spinach, and artichoke dip

This cheesy dish is an indulgence, that's for sure, but there are a few healthy additions here that you won't find in traditional versions of the recipe: chia, whole wheat flour, and shiitake mushrooms, all of which give the dip a fiber boost. Note that I use whole wheat *pastry* flour—it's finer than regular whole wheat flour, which gives it a texture more like white flour. You can also use gluten-free flour in this recipe if you prefer. This recipe is party-size—it will serve about 12 with organic blue corn tortilla chips or whole grain pita chips. Cut it in half if you're serving a smaller group.

MAKES 6 CUPS

1 pound fresh baby spinach

2 tablespoons unsalted butter

1 pound shiitake mushrooms, stems removed, thinly sliced

½ small yellow onion, finely chopped (about ⅓ cup)

½ teaspoon freshly ground black pepper

3 large cloves garlic, peeled and minced

¼ cup whole wheat pastry flour or all-purpose gluten-free flour

2 ¼ cups 2 percent milk

Preheat the oven to 350°F.

Place the spinach in the basket of a steamer and steam until wilted, 2 to 3 minutes. Strain and thoroughly squeeze spinach dry with a clean kitchen towel or cheesecloth. Set aside.

Melt the butter in a large deep nonstick (PFOA-free) skillet over medium heat. Add the mushrooms, onion, and black pepper and sauté until the mushrooms are wilted, about 8 minutes. Add the garlic and sauté until fragrant, about 1 minute. Add the flour and stir briskly for 1 minute. Slowly pour in the milk while stirring continuously until a creamy sauce forms, about 2 minutes. Stir in the chia seeds, lemon juice, salt, hot pepper sauce, and nutmeg. Remove from the heat. Stir in the Parmesan cheese until smooth. Then stir in the quark, artichoke hearts, the reserved spinach, and ⅓ cup of the Monterey Jack cheese until evenly combined. Taste and adjust seasonings.

½ cup black or white chia seeds

1½ tablespoons freshly squeezed lemon juice (from about ½ lemon)

1½ teaspoons sea salt

¾ teaspoon hot pepper sauce

⅛ teaspoon ground or freshly grated nutmeg

½ cup freshly grated Parmesan cheese

⅓ cup quark or sour cream

1 (6.25-ounce) jar marinated artichoke hearts, drained, coarsely chopped

⅔ cup shredded Monterey Jack cheese

Spread dip in a 2-quart baking or oven-safe serving dish. Sprinkle with the remaining ⅓ cup of Monterey Jack cheese. Bake until the cheese is melted and dip is steaming hot, about 15 minutes. Serve warm. If desired, serve with additional hot pepper sauce on the side. For best results, enjoy immediately. Or store in individual microwave-safe bowls, cover, and refrigerate for up to 1 week; gently reheat in the microwave to serve.

roasted tomato compote with chia yogurt cheese

Roasting tomatoes on low heat concentrates their flavor, making them so sweet they taste almost like candy. The yogurt cheese complements the tomatoes' sweetness and, separately, also makes a wonderful breakfast dish or dessert. Serve the combined tomatoes and yogurt cheese with an array of cut-up vegetables, bread, or Gluten-Free Sun-Dried Tomato Chia Crackers (page 66). To serve the yogurt cheese separately for breakfast, simply omit the salt and spoon fresh fruit or Chia-Peach Jam (page 40) on top. You can even spread the yogurt cheese on a bagel (in lieu of cream cheese) and top with smoked salmon.

MAKES 1¹/₂ CUPS COMPOTE AND
ABOUT 2 CUPS YOGURT CHEESE

YOGURT CHEESE

2 cups plain Greek or Icelandic yogurt

2 tablespoons white chia seeds

Pinch of sea salt

TOMATO COMPOTE

2 pints cherry tomatoes, stemmed and cut in half if large

4 cloves garlic, peeled and lightly smashed

3 tablespoons extra-virgin olive oil

Sea salt

Freshly ground black pepper

2 sprigs thyme

1 tablespoon black or white chia seeds

To make the yogurt cheese, the night before you plan to serve the dish, stir together the yogurt, chia seeds, and salt to taste until well combined. Line a colander with cheesecloth or a paper towel and set the colander over a bowl. Spoon the yogurt into the colander, cover with plastic wrap, and place in the refrigerator overnight or for at least 6 to 8 hours.

To make the tomato compote, preheat the oven to 250°F. Line a baking sheet with unbleached parchment paper or aluminum foil.

Toss the tomatoes and garlic with the oil to coat, adding a good pinch of salt and a grinding of pepper. Spread the tomatoes and garlic in a single layer on the prepared baking sheet and tuck in the thyme sprigs. Place in the oven and roast until the tomatoes have collapsed and given up their juices, about

CONTINUED

snacks and small bites

roasted tomato compote with chia yogurt cheese (continued)

1 to 1$\frac{1}{2}$ hours. Remove and stir in the chia seeds. Allow to cool. Discard thyme sprigs.

Remove the yogurt cheese from the refrigerator and discard any whey that has accumulated in the bowl. The yogurt cheese should be thick, the consistency of cream cheese. Turn out the cheese into a serving bowl. Gently peel off the paper towel or cheesecloth and discard.

Serve stirred together in a large bowl, or in two separate bowls for individual spreading. Or cover and store in the refrigerator for up to 3 days.

salads and soups

The dishes in this chapter will take you through all four seasons. Some (like Chia Gazpacho, page 95) are decidedly summery, while others (such as Creamy Coconut Ginger-Carrot Soup, page 96) are fabulous any time of year. One of my first discoveries when experimenting in the kitchen was how wonderfully chia works as an addition to salad dressings and soups. In both cases, the seeds (and their gel) can replace some of the less healthy fats and calories you might ordinarily use, slimming down a dish without sacrificing texture or flavor while boosting the nutrients along the way. That's just another thing I love about chia. I don't like to count calories, but I do like to eat in moderation and know that what I eat is packed with nutrients; adding chia is the perfect way to accomplish both.

raspberry–chia dressed arugula salad with mint and almonds

In recent years, tea has moved out of the teapot and into a host of different dishes. And for good reason: like chia, tea has many antioxidants, so along with adding flavor, it helps up the good-for-you quotient of anything you add it to. Here I use jasmine tea to impart a fragrant, floral essence to this light and refreshing salad.

SERVES 4

½ cup freshly brewed jasmine green or white tea, at room temperature

2 tablespoons freshly squeezed lemon juice (from about 1 small lemon)

2 tablespoons extra-virgin olive oil

1 teaspoon honey or agave nectar

½ teaspoon freshly ground black pepper

¼ teaspoon sea salt

1 (6-ounce) package fresh raspberries

¼ cup white chia seeds

5 cups firmly packed fresh baby arugula (about 5 ounces)

½ large English cucumber, unpeeled and thinly sliced

⅓ cup extra-thin-sliced red onion

¼ cup chopped fresh mint

3 tablespoons sliced natural almonds, toasted

Place the tea, lemon juice, oil, honey, pepper, salt, and ¼ cup of the raspberries in a blender. Cover and puree. Pour into a small bowl, stir in the chia seeds, and let stand for about 20 minutes. (Makes 1⅛ cups raspberry-chia dressing.)

Toss together the arugula, cucumber, onion, and mint in a large bowl. Transfer salad to individual plates or bowls. Taste the raspberry-chia dressing and adjust seasonings. Sprinkle salad with half of the dressing, the remaining raspberries, and the almonds.

Serve with the remaining dressing on the side.

bocconcini and tomato salad
with chia–white balsamic vinaigrette

To me, the combination of mozzarella, tomatoes, and basil is a sure sign that summer has arrived! This salad takes those familiar ingredients (bocconcini are small balls of mozzarella), plus a few unexpected ones (like tea and pine nuts) and tosses them together to create a thoroughly satisfying starter. If you can't find white balsamic vinegar at your local grocery store, the regular red variety will do. Just expect that the cheese will take on a bit of a rosy hue. You can also serve this tasty salad as a main dish; I like to add grilled shrimp or wild salmon to fill it out.

SERVES 4

½ cup freshly brewed green or white tea, at room temperature

¼ cup white chia seeds

2 tablespoons white balsamic vinegar

1 shallot, minced

1 clove garlic, peeled and minced

3 tablespoons extra-virgin olive oil

¼ teaspoon sea salt

¼ teaspoon freshly ground black pepper

6 cups firmly packed mesclun or mixed baby greens (about 6 ounces)

12 cherry tomatoes, thinly sliced

8 ounces bocconcini or diced fresh mozzarella

2 tablespoons thinly sliced fresh basil

3 tablespoons pine nuts, toasted

To make the vinaigrette, place the tea, chia seeds, vinegar, shallot, and garlic in a bowl and whisk to combine. Drizzle in the oil while whisking, then add the salt and pepper. Let stand for about 20 minutes. (Makes 1¼ cups chia–white balsamic vinaigrette.)

Arrange the mesclun on a platter or individual plates. Drizzle with half of the vinaigrette. Sprinkle with the tomatoes, bocconcini, basil, and pine nuts. Serve with the remaining vinaigrette on the side. If you don't use all of the vinaigrette, it keeps well refrigerated in an airtight jar for up to a week.

ancient grains salad
with roasted asparagus

This salad is made with freekeh, an ancient grain made from roasted green wheat. Freekeh has a few things in common with chia: both were largely unknown in the United States until recently, but beloved elsewhere (Mexico and Guatemala in the case of chia, the Middle East and Northern Africa for freekeh). Both are also incredibly rich in protein and fiber.

-------------------------- SERVES 4 --------------------------

1 cup cracked freekeh

3 tablespoons extra-virgin olive oil

¼ cup black or white chia seeds

1 teaspoon sea salt

¼ teaspoon freshly ground black pepper

24 medium asparagus spears, ends trimmed, cut into 1-inch pieces on diagonal

2 tablespoons freshly squeezed lemon juice (from about 1 small lemon)

¼ cup finely diced red onion

1½ tablespoons chopped fresh dill

Cook the freekeh according to package directions; drain. Transfer the cooked freekeh to a bowl and immediately stir in 1½ tablespoons of the oil, the chia seeds, ¾ teaspoon of the salt, and the pepper. Set aside to cool slightly, about 20 minutes, stirring a couple of times. Then chill in the refrigerator.

Meanwhile, preheat the oven to 475°F. Place the asparagus in a single layer on a large rimmed baking sheet, sprinkle with the remaining 1½ tablespoons of oil and ¼ teaspoon of salt, and toss to coat. Roast until crisp-tender, about 10 minutes, shaking pan halfway through cooking time.

Fluff the chilled freekeh with a fork. Stir in asparagus, lemon juice, red onion, and dill. Taste and adjust seasonings, and serve.

farro salad with mizuna, goat cheese, and goji berries

Using chia in grain salads is so simple—no need to make a gel, you just stir the seeds into the grains after they've stopped cooking. Adding chia *before* cooking can result in sticky grains, something to remember when adding chia to other grain-based recipes or developing one of your own.

------- SERVES 6 -------

6 cups purified water

1½ cups whole farro, rinsed and drained

1¾ teaspoons sea salt

¼ cup black or white chia seeds

3 tablespoons extra-virgin olive oil

½ cup dried goji berries, dried cranberries, or finely diced dried unsulfured apricots

½ teaspoon freshly ground black pepper

6 cups firmly packed mizuna or baby salad greens (about 6 ounces)

¼ cup finely chopped fresh basil or mint

¼ cup freshly squeezed lemon juice (from about 1 large lemon)

½ cup shelled lightly salted pistachios

5 ounces soft goat cheese, crumbled

Combine the water, farro, and 1½ teaspoons of the salt in a large saucepan and bring to a boil over high heat. Reduce heat to medium-low, cover, and simmer until farro is desired tenderness, about 40 minutes. Drain well of excess liquid through a fine-mesh strainer.

Transfer the cooked farro to a bowl and immediately stir in the chia seeds, olive oil, goji berries, pepper, and the remaining ¼ teaspoon of salt. Set aside to cool slightly, about 20 minutes, stirring a couple of times. Then chill in the refrigerator.

When the farro is cool and ready to serve, gently stir in the mizuna, basil, lemon juice, and pistachios. Taste and adjust seasonings. Gently stir in or sprinkle with the goat cheese and serve.

purple potato salad
with avocado-chia dressing

Instead of tossing all of the ingredients together in this healthy, mayonnaise-free take on potato salad, the potatoes are served on a bed of the creamy avocado-chia dressing. The contrast of the purple potatoes against the green dressing is a real showstopper. If purple potatoes aren't available, this recipe also works well with red-skinned potatoes.

SERVES 4

1½ pounds baby purple or red creamer potatoes, unpeeled, scrubbed, and quartered

1¼ teaspoons sea salt

½ Hass avocado, pitted, peeled, and diced

2 tablespoons freshly squeezed lemon juice (from about 1 small lemon)

½ cup freshly brewed jasmine green or white tea, at room temperature

2 tablespoons plain yogurt (not Greek yogurt)

¼ cup white chia seeds

1 garlic clove, peeled and minced

Hot pepper sauce

2 green onions, green and white parts, thinly sliced on diagonal

1 medium celery stalk, thinly sliced on diagonal

1 tablespoon finely chopped fresh dill or cilantro

Place the potatoes in a large saucepan and cover with cold water. Add ¾ teaspoon of the salt and bring to a boil over high heat. Cover, reduce heat to medium-low, and cook until potatoes are just tender, about 10 minutes. Drain potatoes, place in a large bowl, and chill in the refrigerator.

In a bowl, thoroughly mash the avocado with the lemon juice until smooth. Add the tea, yogurt, chia seeds, garlic, a few drops of hot pepper sauce, and ¼ teaspoon of the salt and whisk to combine. Let stand for about 20 minutes. (Makes 1¼ cups avocado-chia dressing.)

Remove the potatoes from the refrigerator. Add the green onions, celery, and the remaining ¼ teaspoon of salt to chilled potatoes and gently toss. Smear the avocado-chia dressing onto four salad plates, creating a "bed" for the potato salad. Top with the potato mixture, sprinkle with dill, and serve.

spiced watermelon feta salad

Watermelon is just too luscious to limit its use to fruit salad. Here it's cubed and combined with a feta that provides just the right amount of salty tang.

SERVES 4 TO 6

2 teaspoons black or white chia seeds

1½ tablespoons purified water

½ large watermelon, rind removed and cut into 1-inch cubes and seeded (about 6 cups)

1 cup cherry tomatoes, stemmed and halved

¼ cup freshly squeezed lime juice (from about 2 limes)

2 tablespoons extra-virgin olive oil

Pinch of ground cayenne pepper

¾ teaspoon kosher salt

4 ounces feta cheese

2 tablespoons chopped fresh mint or basil

In a small bowl, stir together the chia seeds and water and let stand for about 20 minutes. (Makes 2 tablespoons chia gel.)

Place the watermelon and cherry tomatoes in a large bowl.

To make the dressing, whisk together the lime juice, chia gel, oil, cayenne, and salt in a small bowl. Taste and adjust seasonings. Toss the watermelon and tomatoes with the lime-chia dressing. Fold in the feta cheese and mint, and serve.

chia gazpacho

Once tomato season hits, I get out my blender and basically keep it at the ready all summer long for making this cold Spanish soup. Adding chia to gazpacho gives it body without changing the flavor. Garnish with croutons, diced cucumber or avocado, chopped hard-boiled egg or almonds (or a mixture of the above) and serve as a meal starter or, in double portions, as a meal itself. I recommend eating gazpacho the day you make it, otherwise the nutrients (especially the vitamin C) start to diminish.

SERVES 8

1/3 cup black or white chia seeds

1 cup purified water

1/4 cup sherry vinegar

1 tablespoon sea salt

2 cucumbers, peeled if desired, cut into chunks

6 large ripe Roma tomatoes (or 4 beefsteak tomatoes), cored and cut into chunks

One small bell pepper, any color, stemmed, seeded, and cut into large pieces

1 large (or 2 small) cloves garlic, peeled and smashed

1 cup ice cubes

1/4 cup extra-virgin olive oil

Place the chia seeds, water, vinegar, salt, cucumbers, tomatoes, bell pepper, garlic, and ice cubes in a blender. Cover and pulse a couple of times to break up the vegetables. Then run the blender to bring the soup to a coarse puree while adding oil in a steady stream.

Transfer to a nonreactive container, cover, chill in the refrigerator until cold, and serve. Or serve at room temperature.

creamy coconut ginger-carrot soup

Coconut milk is a staple in Thai cooking, but you don't have to limit it to Asian food; it's a great resource for making anything super yummy and creamy. I like Native Forest Organic Coconut Milk. To give this velvet soup a tiny bit of crunch and extra visual appeal, chia seeds are stirred in *after* the soup is pureed.

SERVES 4

1 (13.5-ounce) can coconut milk

1 medium yellow onion, chopped

¾ teaspoon sea salt

2 teaspoons peeled, grated fresh ginger

2 teaspoons Thai yellow or red curry paste

1 clove garlic, peeled and chopped

12 ounces baby carrots, quartered lengthwise

2¾ cups low-sodium vegetable broth, plus more as needed

2 tablespoons freshly squeezed lime juice (from about 1 lime)

15 large cilantro sprigs plus 5 small cilantro sprigs

¼ cup plus 1 teaspoon black or white chia seeds

Heat ⅓ cup of the coconut milk in a large saucepan over medium-high heat. Add the onion and salt and cook while stirring until onion is softened, about 5 minutes. Stir in the ginger, curry paste, and garlic and cook while stirring until well combined and fragrant, about 1 minute.

Add the carrots, 2¾ cups of broth, the lime juice, the 15 large cilantro sprigs, and the remaining coconut milk and bring to a boil over high heat. Reduce heat to low and simmer, covered, until the carrots are very tender, about 30 minutes. Remove the cilantro sprigs and puree soup in batches in a blender, using the hot fill line as a guide.

Transfer the pureed soup to a clean saucepan and place over low heat. Stir in ¼ cup of the chia seeds and simmer uncovered until chia seeds are fully hydrated and soup reaches desired consistency, about 20 minutes, stirring occasionally. (Note: If soup becomes thicker than you desire, stir in additional vegetable broth by the tablespoon to reach ideal consistency.) Taste and adjust seasonings, garnish with the remaining 1 teaspoon of chia seeds and small cilantro sprigs, and serve.

main dishes

From lunchtime sandwiches to dinner-worthy pastas and stews, these main dishes deliver an array of different flavors—they'll have you traveling from India to Greece and many places in between. As someone who loves international travel, it's a joy to bring a taste of these amazing cultures into my kitchen and pair them with chia. I think you'll see that, once again, chia offers versatility, whether it's adding lightness to turkey meatballs or providing crunch as a coating for grilled tofu.

grilled veggie sandwich
with chia dijon-balsamic spread

This is a recipe you can really play with. It's a great way to use leftover grilled veggies—feel free to replace the zucchini and onion with any other cooked vegetables you have on hand—and you can also add sliced turkey or cheese to the mix if you want an even heartier sandwich. The Chia Dijon-Balsamic Spread is great to have around for other uses, so double or triple the recipe as needed and store in an airtight container in the refrigerator for up to a week.

SERVES 2

CHIA DIJON-BALSAMIC SPREAD

2 tablespoons black or white chia seeds

4 teaspoons aged balsamic vinegar

2 teaspoons Dijon mustard

2 teaspoons purified water

1 yellow squash or zucchini, cut lengthwise into 10 slices

2 large slices red onion (not separated into rings)

4 teaspoons extra-virgin olive oil

1/4 teaspoon freshly ground black pepper

1/8 teaspoon sea salt

4 large slices whole grain bread, toasted

1/2 avocado, sliced

12 thin diagonal slices English cucumber or 1 cup baby arugula

To make the spread, in a small bowl, whisk together the chia seeds, vinegar, mustard, and water. Let stand for about 20 minutes. (Makes 2 tablespoons spread.)

Prepare an indoor or outdoor grill. Brush the yellow squash and onion with oil. Grill over medium-high heat until dark grill marks form and veggies are just cooked through, about 4 minutes per side. Sprinkle with pepper and salt. Separate onion into rings.

Spread the chia Dijon-balsamic mixture onto all four slices of toast. Arrange the avocado on two slices of the toast and top with grilled onion, cucumber, grilled yellow squash, and the remaining slices of toast. Cut in half on the diagonal using serrated bread knife and serve.

spicy vegetarian korma with cashews

Based on an Indian classic, this korma gets extra body and texture from chia. The recipe calls for squash, green beans, and mushrooms, but can be made with any of your favorite vegetables. Garam masala can be found in Indian markets or purchased online. Serve with brown basmati rice or whole grain naan.

---- SERVES 4 ----

1½ tablespoons virgin coconut oil

1 medium red onion, finely chopped

½ Thai chile pepper or 1 serrano pepper, minced

2 tablespoons no-salt-added creamy cashew or almond butter

1 tablespoon peeled, grated ginger

2 large cloves garlic, peeled and minced

1 (15-ounce) can no-salt-added tomato sauce

1½ cups low-sodium vegetable broth

1 tablespoon garam masala curry paste

2 teaspoons ground coriander

1¼ teaspoons sea salt

½ teaspoon ground turmeric

2 cups ½-inch-cubed butternut squash or sweet potato

2 cups fresh green beans, cut into 1-inch pieces, or bite-size broccoli florets

2 large portobello mushroom caps, cut into ½-inch-wide slices

¾ cup coconut milk

¼ cup black or white chia seeds

½ cup unsalted raw cashews

¼ cup coarsely chopped fresh cilantro

Heat the oil in a large deep nonstick (PFOA-free) skillet or Dutch oven over medium heat. Add the onion and chile pepper and sauté until onion is softened, about 8 minutes. Add the cashew butter, ginger, and garlic and stir until well combined and fragrant, about 1 minute. Add the tomato sauce, broth, curry paste, coriander, salt, and turmeric and cook while stirring until mixture comes to a simmer, about 5 minutes.

Add the butternut squash, green beans, mushrooms, coconut milk, and chia seeds to the mixture and bring to a boil over high heat. Reduce heat to medium-low and simmer, covered, until the butternut squash is just tender, 20 to 25 minutes, stirring a few times during the simmering process. Stir in the cashews and 2 tablespoons of the cilantro. Taste and adjust seasonings.

Ladle the korma into a serving bowl or individual bowls, sprinkle with the remaining 2 tablespoons of cilantro, and serve.

grilled tofu skewers with chia soy-ginger sauce

Chia is used in two ways here: as part of the marinade and sprinkled on after grilling to add some texture (the tofu will be dry after grilling so the seeds stay dry instead of gelling). Two skewers make a nice entrée served on a bed of greens or rice. You can serve these individually as appetizers, too.

SERVES 4

CHIA SOY-GINGER SAUCE

2 tablespoons brown rice vinegar

2 tablespoons tamari soy sauce

1 tablespoon peeled, grated fresh ginger

1 tablespoon agave nectar or honey

1 tablespoon toasted sesame oil

1 tablespoon black chia seeds

¼ teaspoon red pepper flakes

1 green onion, green and white parts separated, minced or thinly sliced

1 (14-ounce) package extra-firm tofu, drained and squeezed of excess liquid

1 tablespoon black chia seeds

To make the sauce, in a liquid measuring cup or small bowl, whisk together the vinegar, soy sauce, ginger, agave nectar, oil, chia seeds, red pepper flakes, and white part of the green onion. Reserve green parts for garnish. Set aside for 10 minutes to allow seeds to partially hydrate. (Makes ½ cup chia soy-ginger sauce.)

Cut the tofu lengthwise into 4 slices, then cut each slice in half lengthwise, creating 8 long slices. Pour the sauce into a 9 by 13-inch nonreactive pan or similar-size dish. Place the tofu slices in a single layer in the sauce and marinate about 30 minutes, turning over halfway through the marinating time.

Prepare an outdoor or indoor grill. Carefully transfer each tofu slice to the grill using tongs, reserving the sauce. Grill over direct medium-high heat until rich grill marks form on two sides, about 4 minutes per side. Meanwhile, strain the remaining chia soy-ginger sauce through a fine-mesh strainer and reserve the sauce.

Insert skewers into the cooked tofu and arrange on a platter. Sprinkle with 1 tablespoon chia seeds and the green part of the green onion. Serve warm with soy-ginger sauce on the side.

tuscan white beans and baby kale

If you like to have dinner on the table in less than twenty minutes, this is your dish: there's very little prep work (it calls for canned beans, although you can always use home-cooked beans if you prefer) and it cooks up quickly. Serve it on its own as a vegetarian main dish, or as a bed for roasted chicken or sausage. This recipe works fine with regular kale (just remove spines and chop before using) as well as baby spinach and Swiss chard, too.

SERVES 3 AS AN ENTRÉE OR 6 AS A SIDE DISH

2 tablespoons extra-virgin olive oil

1 small (or 1/2 large) red onion, diced

2 large cloves garlic, peeled and minced

5 cups packed fresh baby kale (about 5 ounces)

3/4 teaspoon sea salt

1/2 teaspoon freshly ground black pepper

1/8 teaspoon red pepper flakes

1 1/2 cups low-sodium vegetable broth

1/4 cup black or white chia seeds

1 teaspoon fresh lemon juice or white balsamic vinegar

1/2 teaspoon finely chopped fresh rosemary or thyme

1 (15-ounce) can cannellini beans, drained, or 1 1/2 cups freshly cooked

1/4 cup chopped fresh flat-leaf parsley

Heat the oil in a nonstick (PFOA-free) Dutch oven or large deep skillet over medium-high heat. Add the onion and sauté until softened, about 5 minutes. Add the garlic and sauté until fragrant, about 30 seconds. Stir in the kale, salt, black pepper, red pepper flakes, broth, chia seeds, lemon juice, and rosemary and bring to a boil over high heat. Reduce heat to medium and cook uncovered while stirring occasionally until kale is tender, about 5 minutes.

Add the beans and cook, stirring occasionally, until beans are fully heated, about 3 minutes. Stir in the parsley, taste and adjust seasonings, then serve.

black bean and yam enchilada bake

Mexican restaurants tend to limit the choice of enchiladas to cheese, chicken, or beef (with sometimes a crab enchilada thrown in). In other words, there are few choices when you want to eat vegetarian. This enchilada bake extends the options, using garnet yams (sometimes also called red yams) as a base. The chia in this recipe is mixed with salsa and lime juice to make a tangy topping. As a rule, I always try to use non-GMO corn and corn tortillas.

------------------------------- SERVES 8 -------------------------------

2 large (11-ounce) unpeeled garnet yams or white sweet potatoes, scrubbed and cut into 1/2-inch cubes

1 cup frozen corn, thawed

1 small (or 1/2 large) red onion, cut into large dice

3 tablespoons extra-virgin olive oil

3/4 teaspoon sea salt

1/4 teaspoon ground cumin

1/4 teaspoon ground cinnamon

1 cup salsa verde (tomatillo sauce)

1/4 cup black or white chia seeds

1 tablespoon freshly squeezed lime juice (from about 1/2 lime)

1 (15-ounce) can black beans, drained

8 ounces goat cheese, crumbled

Preheat the oven to 425°F.

Stir together the yams, corn, onion, oil, 1/2 teaspoon of the salt, cumin, and cinnamon in a large bowl. Arrange in a single layer on a large rimmed baking sheet and roast, stirring occasionally, until all of the vegetables are lightly caramelized and the yams are tender, 25 to 30 minutes. Remove from oven and set aside. Lower oven temperature to 350°F.

In a liquid measuring cup or small bowl, whisk together the salsa, chia seeds, and lime juice and let stand for about 20 minutes. Set aside. (Makes 1 1/4 cups salsa-chia mixture.)

Gently stir together the beans, goat cheese, 1 cup of the Monterey Jack cheese, and garlic in a bowl. Set aside.

In a liquid measuring cup or small bowl, whisk together the broth, 1/2 cup of the sour cream, and the remaining 1/4 teaspoon of salt. Set aside.

2 cups shredded Monterey Jack cheese (about 8 ounces)

2 large garlic cloves, peeled and minced

½ cup low-sodium vegetable broth

1 cup sour cream

18 (6-inch-diameter) corn tortillas

¼ cup coarsely chopped fresh cilantro

Arrange 6 of the tortillas in a 9 by 13-inch baking dish. Brush with ½ cup of the creamy broth. Evenly top with half of the vegetable mixture and half of the bean-cheese mixture. Arrange 6 more tortillas. Brush with the remaining ½ cup of creamy broth. Evenly top with the remaining vegetable mixture and bean-cheese mixture. Arrange the remaining 6 tortillas on top and press to pack layers. Evenly spread the salsa-chia mixture on top of the tortillas. Sprinkle with the remaining 1 cup of Monterey Jack cheese.

Bake until enchilada dish is heated through and cheeses are fully melted, 25 to 30 minutes. Remove from oven and let stand at least 5 minutes to complete the cooking process. Cut into 8 portions. Dollop with the remaining ½ cup of sour cream, sprinkle with the cilantro, and serve.

shrimp skewers with chia romesco sauce

Romesco sauce is a thick, smoky sauce that's a staple in Spain and wonderful dolloped or spread on everything from potatoes to shrimp. Some versions have bread in them, but this one uses chia as a thickener. For a richer-tasting sauce, replace half the almonds with hazelnuts.

ROMESCO SAUCE

1 tablespoon black or white chia seeds

2 tablespoons purified water

1 cup raw almonds

3 large red bell peppers

1 large Roma tomato

2 medium cloves garlic, unpeeled

1 teaspoon Aleppo chile flakes or ancho chile powder

1 tablespoon Spanish smoked paprika

3 tablespoons sherry vinegar

Pinch of sea salt

1/3 cup extra-virgin olive oil

1 pound large shrimp, peeled and deveined

1 1/2 tablespoons extra-virgin olive oil

1/4 teaspoon sea salt

Preheat the oven to 350°F.

To make the sauce, in a small bowl, whisk together the chia seeds and water and let stand for about 20 minutes. (Makes 3 tablespoons thick chia gel.)

Spread the almonds out on a baking sheet and toast in the oven, stirring, for about 10 minutes or until hot and fragrant. Transfer to a plate to cool.

Turn the oven to broil. Place the whole bell peppers, tomato, and garlic cloves on the baking sheet and broil, turning frequently and watching carefully, until vegetables are blackened and softened. Transfer the peppers to a bowl and cover with aluminum foil. Let stand for about 10 minutes.

Meanwhile, remove skins from the garlic and add to a food processor. Rub the skin off the tomato, cut out the core, and add the flesh to the food processor. Add the chia gel, chile flakes, paprika, vinegar, and salt to the food processor along with the almonds.

When the peppers are cool enough to handle, remove blackened skins, seeds, and stems, capturing all the juices in a bowl. Add flesh and juices to the food processor. Pulse to chop the nuts, then keep the processor on as you drizzle in the 1/3 cup of olive oil in a steady stream until a thick puree forms. Taste and adjust seasonings. Transfer to a small serving bowl and set aside.

Prepare an outdoor or indoor grill. Thread the shrimp onto metal or water-soaked bamboo skewers. Rub the shrimp with the olive oil and sprinkle with sea salt. Grill over medium heat until just pink and opaque, 5 to 7 minutes. Serve shrimp skewers with the romesco sauce alongside.

grilled halibut with chia pesto

If you're looking to increase your intake of omega-3s, you can't do better than to have a meal that combines chia with fish, especially halibut (Alaskan halibut in particular is one of your best seafood sources of omega-3s). The tasty pesto that tops off this dish is also delicious tossed with pasta.

SERVES 2

CHIA PESTO

1 tablespoon black or white chia seeds

3 tablespoons purified water

1/2 cup walnuts

1/4 cup pine nuts or almonds

2 large cloves garlic, peeled and smashed

1 bunch fresh basil, leaves only (about 4 firmly packed cups)

1 1/4 teaspoons sea salt

1/4 teaspoon freshly ground black pepper

3/4 cup extra-virgin olive oil

2 (7-ounce) halibut fillets, about 1 inch thick

1 tablespoon extra-virgin olive oil

To make the pesto, in a small bowl, whisk together the chia seeds and water and let stand for about 20 minutes. (Makes 1/4 cup thick chia gel.)

Place the walnuts, pine nuts, garlic, chia gel, basil, 1 teaspoon of the salt, and the pepper in a food processor or powerful blender. Pulse to coarsely chop. Keep processor on as you drizzle in the olive oil in a steady stream until incorporated. Taste and adjust seasonings. Reserve 1/4 cup of pesto and refrigerate the remainder in an airtight container for up to 3 days to toss with pasta for another meal. Or freeze for up to 3 months for later use.

Prepare an indoor or outdoor grill. Brush the fish with the 1 tablespoon oil and place skin side up on grill. Close the lid and grill over medium-high heat for approximately 4 minutes. Carefully turn the fish over, skin side down, and cook until fish is just opaque, about 6 more minutes. Transfer the fish to a plate, sprinkle with the remaining 1/4 teaspoon of salt, cover loosely with aluminum foil, and let stand for about 5 minutes to finish the cooking process.

Top halibut with a spoonful of the reserved pesto and serve.

salmon on brioche with chia tzatziki

Tzatziki is the Greek answer to the Indian yogurt side dish raita (see page 75), only with garlic and dill as the lead flavors. Its aromatic tang is the perfect complement to salmon's rich flavor. This chia-spiked version is thicker than traditional tzatziki, making it a great spread for pita-bread sandwiches and even a substitute for mayonnaise in tuna salad. You'll likely have about $1/2$ cup tzatziki left over, which can be covered and refrigerated for up to a week.

------------------------------ SERVES 4 ------------------------------

CHIA TZATZIKI SPREAD

$3/4$ cup plain yogurt (not Greek)

$1/4$ cup white chia seeds

$1/4$ cup coarsely grated cucumber

1 tablespoon chopped fresh dill

1 tablespoon extra-virgin olive oil

2 teaspoons fresh lemon juice

1 clove garlic, peeled and minced

$1/4$ teaspoon sea salt

4 (3.5-ounce) skin-on salmon fillets (cut about the length of a hot dog bun)

1 teaspoon extra-virgin olive oil

$1/4$ teaspoon sea salt

$1/4$ teaspoon freshly ground black pepper

$1/4$ teaspoon ground cumin

4 brioche or whole grain hot dog buns, split

1 cup shredded romaine lettuce

$1/4$ cup finely diced red onion

To make the spread, in a liquid measuring cup or small bowl, whisk together the yogurt, chia seeds, cucumber, dill, oil, lemon juice, garlic, and salt and let stand for about 20 minutes.

Prepare an outdoor or indoor grill. Brush or rub the salmon with the oil and sprinkle with the salt, pepper, and cumin. Grill salmon skin side up over direct medium-high heat for $3 1/2$ minutes, then flip over and grill until the skin is crisp and the fish is just cooked through, $2 1/2$ to 3 minutes more. Remove skin. Meanwhile, toast the buns on the grill, if desired.

Spread buns with the chia tzatziki mixture. Layer the lettuce, salmon, and onion in the buns and serve.

mediterranean pasta with tuna

When buying canned tuna, I look for brands using fish caught by sustainable methods—meaning that catching the tuna doesn't bring in other fish and animals by accident. Wild Planet is a good choice, but there are other ocean-friendly options: just look for line- or pole-caught albacore. This recipe makes a generous amount; leftovers can be served at room temperature for lunch the next day. I use gluten-free brown rice noodles, but it works with whole wheat pasta, too.

1 pound brown rice fusilli

¼ cup extra-virgin olive oil

1 yellow onion, finely chopped

¼ teaspoon sea salt

3 cloves garlic, peeled and thinly sliced

½ cup dry white wine or low-sodium vegetable broth

6 sun-dried tomato halves, slivered

2 medium vine-ripened tomatoes, cored and chopped

2 (5-ounce) cans tuna, drained

⅓ cup drained capers

⅓ cup prepared tapenade or ½ cup pitted olives, finely chopped

¼ cup white chia seeds

1 cup purified water

3 tablespoons chopped fresh parsley

1 teaspoon grated lemon zest

¼ teaspoon freshly ground black pepper

Pinch of red pepper flakes (optional)

Bring a large pot of salted water to a boil. Add the pasta and cook until just shy of al dente, or 1 minute less than package directions.

While the pasta is cooking, heat the olive oil over medium heat in a large deep sauté pan. Add the onion and salt and sauté until onion is softened and golden, about 5 minutes. Add the garlic and sauté until fragrant, about 1 minute. Add the wine to deglaze the pan. Add the sun-dried tomatoes, fresh tomatoes, tuna, capers, tapenade, chia seeds, and water. Cover and simmer until juices are thickened and chia seeds are hydrated, about 5 minutes.

Drain the pasta, reserving 1 cup of the pasta cooking water. Add the drained pasta to the sauce in the sauté pan, tossing to coat evenly. Add pasta water by the tablespoon to smooth out the sauce and help it bind. Add the parsley, lemon zest, black pepper, and red pepper flakes and toss to combine. Taste, adjust seasonings, and serve.

main dishes

mole-style chicken stew

Living in California, I'm lucky enough to be surrounded by incredible Mexican food. That was the inspiration for this flavorful stew packed with protein and spices and some of my favorite flavors like chiles and warm, earthy cumin. The recipe calls for an entire chicken cut up into 10 pieces, but you can also use 3 pounds of hindquarters or thighs if you prefer. Either way, I suggest buying free-range, organic chicken and using bone-in pieces for the best flavor. Mole traditionally has ingredients that may seem unusual in a savory sauce—prunes, almond butter, and chocolate, among them—but trust me, they all blend together beautifully.

SERVES 6

1 (3-pound) chicken, cut into 10 pieces

2 teaspoons kosher salt plus additional for seasoning chicken

½ teaspoon freshly ground black pepper

3 tablespoons extra-virgin olive oil

1 teaspoon cumin seeds

1 medium yellow onion, chopped

4 cloves garlic, peeled and chopped

3 tablespoons chili powder

1 tablespoon ground chipotle chile

1 teaspoon dried oregano

½ cup prunes (dried plums), minced or ground to a paste in a food processor

Pat the chicken dry and season well with salt and pepper. Heat the olive oil over medium-high heat in a large Dutch oven. Brown the chicken, in batches if necessary, until deeply golden. Using tongs or a fork, transfer the chicken to a plate. Cover with aluminum foil to keep warm. Reserve leftover fat in the Dutch oven.

Add the cumin seeds to the Dutch oven and fry until fragrant, about 30 seconds. Add the onion and garlic along with the 2 teaspoons of salt. Sauté, stirring frequently, until the onion is softened and golden. Add the chili powder, ground chipotle, oregano, and prunes, mixing well. Add the tomatoes and cook until slightly caramelized. Stir in the rice and chia seeds.

1 (28-ounce) can plum tomatoes

1 cup brown basmati rice

1/3 cup black chia seeds

1 cinnamon stick

2 cans white beans, rinsed and drained

2 ounces unsweetened or bittersweet chocolate, grated

2 tablespoons almond butter

2 Hass avocados, for serving

Fresh chopped cilantro, for serving

Transfer the chicken pieces to the Dutch oven, and then add enough water to cover the chicken by an inch. Add the cinnamon stick and beans. Bring to a boil, then lower to a simmer and cook until the chicken is tender and broth is flavorful, about 20 minutes. Whisk in the chocolate and almond butter, taste, and adjust seasonings.

Peel and dice the avocados. Ladle the stew into deep bowls, top with the avocado and cilantro, and serve.

linguine al limone with grilled chia-chicken meatballs

Chia gel replaces eggs in this recipe, helping keep these chicken meatballs light and fluffy. The sauce is creamy and lemony, a combination that simply melts in the mouth. As an option, try spinach linguine, which pairs nicely with the flavors in this dish and looks beautiful.

SERVES 4

¼ cup white chia seeds

½ cup purified water

1 pound ground chicken

¾ cup rolled (old-fashioned) oats

⅓ cup coarsely grated or minced red onion

⅓ cup plus ¼ cup grated Parmigiano-Reggiano cheese

3 tablespoons extra-virgin olive oil

¼ cup finely chopped fresh flat-leaf parsley

1 teaspoon finely chopped fresh oregano, or ½ teaspoon dried oregano

2 cloves garlic, peeled and minced

1½ teaspoons sea salt

1 teaspoon freshly ground black pepper

½ teaspoon red pepper flakes

12 ounces whole grain linguine

⅓ cup half-and-half

Juice and zest of 1 large lemon

2 tablespoons thinly sliced or chopped fresh basil (optional)

In a liquid measuring cup or small bowl, whisk together the chia seeds and water and let stand for about 20 minutes. (Makes ¾ cup extra-thick chia gel.)

Prepare an indoor or outdoor grill, or preheat the oven to 475°F.

In a large bowl, use your hands to evenly combine the chia gel, ground chicken, oats, onion, ¼ cup of the cheese, 2 tablespoons of the olive oil, the parsley, oregano, garlic, 1 teaspoon of the salt, ½ teaspoon of the black pepper, and the red pepper flakes. When evenly combined, firmly form mixture into 20 meatballs (about 3 tablespoons each).

Grill over medium heat until well done and brown on all sides, about 15 minutes, rotating only as needed. Alternatively, line a large rimmed baking sheet with aluminum foil and coat with cooking spray. Arrange the meatballs on the baking sheet and roast until well done, about 20 minutes. Insert 4 (10-inch) skewers into cooked meatballs, 5 meatballs each. If necessary, keep warm in 175°F oven while preparing linguine.

CONTINUED

main dishes

117

linguine al limone with grilled chia-chicken meatballs (continued)

Cook the linguine according to package directions. Drain the pasta, reserving $3/4$ cup pasta cooking water.

Bring the half-and-half, the remaining 1 tablespoon of oil, and reserved pasta water to a boil over high heat in a large saucepan. Add the drained pasta and toss to combine. Add the lemon juice and toss to combine. Add the remaining $1/3$ cup of cheese, $1/2$ teaspoon of salt, and $1/2$ teaspoon of black pepper and toss to combine.

Transfer the linguine to four large pasta bowls. Top each with a skewer of chicken meatballs, sprinkle with basil and lemon zest, and serve.

thai-style sweet-and-sour chicken thighs

The balance of three flavors—sour, sweet, and salty—are what make Thai dishes so irresistible. These succulent chicken thighs get their tang from lime juice, their sweetness from agave nectar (or honey if you prefer), and their saltiness from soy. Red pepper flakes add a touch of heat. Pair them with sautéed broccoli, green beans, or bok choy.

SERVES 4

1/4 cup freshly squeezed lime juice (from about 2 limes)

1/4 cup purified water

1/4 cup black or white chia seeds

2 tablespoons agave nectar or honey

1 teaspoon tamari soy sauce

1 teaspoon sea salt

8 chicken thighs on bone with skin

1/2 teaspoon red pepper flakes

2 tablespoons unrefined peanut oil

1/4 cup coarsely chopped fresh cilantro

In a liquid measuring cup or small bowl, whisk together the lime juice, water, chia seeds, agave nectar, soy sauce, and 1/4 teaspoon of the salt and let stand for about 20 minutes. (Makes about 3/4 cup lime-chia dressing.)

Sprinkle the chicken with the remaining 3/4 teaspoon of salt and the red pepper flakes.

Heat the oil in a large nonstick (PFOA-free) skillet over medium-high heat. Place the chicken thighs, skin side down, in the pan and cook until skin is brown, about 10 minutes. Reduce heat to medium and carefully flip over each piece of chicken (skin has a tendency to stick to the skillet so pull gently). Cook, partially covered, until chicken is well done, 8 to 10 minutes.

Transfer thighs to a platter, dress with half of the lime-chia dressing, and sprinkle with cilantro. Serve the remaining lime-chia dressing on the side to dress accompanying vegetables—or enjoy as additional sauce for the chicken.

desserts, sweet nibbles, and cocktails

Can you indulge and eat healthfully at the same time? These desserts and drinks prove that you can. While sweets and cocktails usually provide "empty" calories, the recipes here are spiked with nutrient-rich ingredients that enhance well-being. And as you try them out, you'll notice how easy it is to add chia to desserts and drinks. Chia gel can replace some of the other liquid or eggs in virtually any baked good, and it boosts the consistency and beauty—all those lovely seeds floating around—of any cocktail.

figs with blue cheese and almonds

Fig season varies by region, but whenever they arrive in your neck of the woods, seize the day! Interestingly, figs are actually flowers (the seeds are the actual fruit), which, to me, just adds to their allure. Both dark purple and light green fig varieties are rich in fiber and potassium, and are best bought when slightly soft and eaten within a day or two. Here, for a dessert dish (or even a rich appetizer), I've paired them with blue cheese, a lovely pungent balance to the figs' sweetness. Chia might seem like an afterthought—it's sprinkled on top of the figs—but it actually adds crunch and looks beautiful, nicely finishing the dish.

-------- MAKES 24 --------

2 ounces blue cheese

12 fresh black Mission or Calimyrna figs, stems removed, halved lengthwise

24 almonds, toasted

2 tablespoons black chia seeds

1/2 teaspoon fresh thyme leaves

2 tablespoons honey

1/8 teaspoon freshly ground black pepper

Press about 1/2 teaspoon blue cheese into the center flesh of each fig. Top each with 1 almond, and arrange figs cut side up on a serving platter.

Sprinkle figs evenly with chia seeds and thyme leaves, drizzle with honey, and sprinkle with pepper. Serve immediately.

chia plum leather

Fruit leather is something most people buy premade, but it's actually easy to make yourself, and your homemade version will be even healthier than store-bought: chia thickens the fruit so you can avoid adding a lot of sugar. Be aware that drying the fruit takes 9 to 10 hours, but you can just stash it in the oven and forget about it (for a while—don't forget it's in there!). The proportions of this recipe work with a variety of different fruits (it's best to use very ripe, even overripe fruit), so you can experiment using all your favorites.

MAKES 8 FRUIT LEATHER ROLLS

12 very ripe plums, pits removed

2 ½ tablespoons milled (ground) chia seeds

Pinch of ground cardamom

2 to 3 tablespoons coconut or date palm sugar

2 tablespoons vegetable oil or nonstick cooking spray

Place the plums, chia, cardamom, and sugar in a food processor or powerful blender. Cover and process until smooth. Let stand for about 20 minutes.

Preheat the oven to 140°F.

Line two baking sheets with unbleached parchment paper and lightly oil. Divide the mixture between sheets and, using a spatula, spread thinly, to about ⅛-inch thickness. For best results, spread fruit evenly, making sure edges are the same thickness as the middle.

Bake until a corner peels easily off the parchment and leather is only slightly tacky to the touch, 9 to 10 hours. Cool, cut into 8 strips, and roll. Store in an airtight container at room temperature. The fruit leather keeps for months.

desserts, sweet nibbles, and cocktails

coconut-cranberry chocolate truffles

With their combination of chia, walnuts, dates, cocoa, and cranberries, these no-guilt truffles are the most nutritious sweets going. Once you get the basic steps down, experiment with different ratios of nuts, try rolling the truffles in whole chia seeds instead of shredded coconut, or swap out the cranberries for chopped dried apricots or other dried fruit.

MAKES 2 DOZEN 1-INCH TRUFFLES

1/2 cup walnuts

1 cup almond meal

1/3 cup black or white chia seeds

2 tablespoons purified water

1 cup firmly packed pitted dates

1/3 cup unsweetened cacao powder

3 tablespoons coconut butter

1/2 cup dried unsweetened cranberries

2 tablespoons cacao nibs

1 cup desiccated, shredded, unsweetened coconut

Place the walnuts, almond meal, and chia seeds in a food processor. Cover and pulse until the walnuts are finely ground. Add the water, dates, cacao powder, and coconut butter. Process until smooth, 1 to 2 minutes. Add the cranberries and cacao nibs. Pulse just to incorporate. Pinch a bit of the mixture between your fingers. It should stick together like pie dough. If it's too crumbly, sprinkle in a bit more water or add a tiny spoonful more coconut butter and pulse a few more times.

Roll the mixture between your palms into 1-inch balls. Evenly spread the coconut on a plate and roll the balls in the coconut to coat. Store in an airtight container for up to 1 week or the freezer for up to 3 months.

pb&j cookies

In a sandwich, delightful; in a cookie, even better! There's a reason peanut butter and jelly is a beloved combination. Here it's baked into oaty rounds with a jammy center, which also happen to be free of gluten, refined sugar, and eggs. The end result is a sweet treat that you'll feel good about serving.

MAKES 18 COOKIES

1 cup fresh raspberries or strawberries

2 tablespoons black or white chia seeds

3 tablespoons purified water

1/2 cup natural peanut butter

1/2 cup coconut or date palm sugar

1/2 cup all-purpose gluten-free flour

1/2 teaspoon cinnamon

1/2 teaspoon baking powder

Pinch of sea salt

3/4 cup gluten-free rolled oats

Place the berries and 1 tablespoon of the chia seeds in a food processor. Cover and process until combined. Transfer to a small bowl and let stand for about 20 minutes.

In a liquid measuring cup or small bowl, whisk together the water and the remaining 1 tablespoon of chia and let stand for about 20 minutes. (Makes 1/4 cup thick chia gel.)

Preheat the oven to 375°F. Line a baking sheet with aluminum foil or unbleached parchment paper.

In a mixing bowl, beat together the chia gel, peanut butter, and sugar until smooth. Sift or whisk together the flour, cinnamon, baking powder, and salt in a large bowl. Add the peanut butter mixture along with the oats and stir until combined. Roll the mixture into 18 balls, about 1 inch diameter each, and place at least 1 inch apart on the baking sheet. After all the balls are placed, wet your thumb and make an indentation in the middle of each cookie. Spoon about 1/2 to 1 teaspoon of the jam in each indentation. (Any leftover jam can be used as a spread for toast or spooned over plain yogurt.) Bake until cookies and jam are set, 12 to 15 minutes. Cool on baking sheet for 1 minute. Then, using a thin spatula, transfer cookies to a wire rack to cool completely. Store in an airtight container for up to 1 week.

gluten-free chocolate almond cookies

These chunky cookies offer intense chocolate almond flavor with just a hint of coconut from the coconut oil. I am a big fan of almond butter, but you can substitute any nut butter, according to your own preferences—try hazelnut, walnut, or peanut.

MAKES 18 COOKIES

1 tablespoon black or white chia seeds

3 tablespoons purified water

1/2 cup almond butter

2 tablespoons virgin coconut oil, coconut butter, or softened butter

2 tablespoons unsweetened cacao powder

1/2 cup coconut palm sugar or date sugar

1/2 teaspoon baking powder

Pinch of sea salt

1 1/2 cups rolled (old-fashioned) oats (or 3/4 cup oats and 3/4 cup quinoa flakes)

1 large egg

In a liquid measuring cup or small bowl, whisk together the chia seeds and water and let stand for about 20 minutes. (Makes 1/4 cup thick chia gel.)

Preheat the oven to 350°F. Line a baking sheet with aluminum foil or unbleached parchment paper.

Place the chia gel, almond butter, and coconut oil in a large mixing bowl and whisk to combine. Sprinkle evenly with the cacao, sugar, baking powder, and salt and whisk to combine. Add the oats and egg and mix thoroughly.

Roll into 18 balls, about 1-inch diameter each, and place 1 inch apart on the baking sheet, flattening the balls slightly as you go. Bake until cookies are set, 12 to 15 minutes. Transfer cookies with foil to the counter to cool for 1 minute. Then, using a thin spatula, transfer cookies to a wire rack to cool completely. Store in an airtight container at room temperature for up to 1 week or in the freezer for up to 3 months.

key lime chia cheesecake

Although this sweet-tart cheesecake is great with a homemade graham cracker crust, which you can whip up pretty quickly, to make this easy cheesecake even easier, use a 9-inch ready-to-use all-natural graham cracker piecrust. If you like a limier flavor, add a teaspoon of lime zest to the batter (which you can sample before cooking because, thanks to chia, there are no raw eggs to worry about).

SERVES 6

GRAHAM CRACKER PIECRUST

6 ounces all-natural or organic graham crackers

2 tablespoons virgin coconut oil or melted unsalted butter

2 teaspoons honey or agave nectar

3 tablespoons freshly squeezed Key lime or regular lime juice (from about 4 1/2 Key limes or 1 1/2 limes)

1/4 cup white chia seeds

1/4 cup purified water

10 ounces Neufchâtel (light cream cheese), at room temperature

1/4 cup raw sugar

1 teaspoon pure vanilla extract

1/8 teaspoon sea salt

Preheat the oven to 350°F.

Place the graham crackers in a food processor. Pulse until coarsely crumbled. Add the oil and honey and blend until finely crumbled. Pour into a standard 9-inch pie pan, pressing firmly to cover the bottom and sides of the pan. Bake until fragrant and firm, about 10 minutes. Transfer the pan to a wire rack to cool completely before filling.

Lower oven to 325°F.

In a liquid measuring cup or small bowl, whisk together the Key lime juice, 3 1/2 tablespoons of the chia seeds, and water and let stand for about 20 minutes. (Makes 2/3 cup lime-chia gel.)

In a large bowl, with an electric mixer on medium speed, mix together the Neufchâtel, sugar, vanilla, and salt until smooth. Add the lime-chia gel and blend until well combined. Pour the batter into the crust and shake gently to settle. Bake until center is nearly set, about 25 minutes.

CONTINUED

HONEY WHIPPED CREAM

¹/₂ cup heavy whipping cream, well chilled

1 tablespoon honey or agave nectar

6 thin slices Key lime or small lime

Cool in the pan on a wire rack. Transfer to the refrigerator until well chilled, at least 3 hours.

Once the cheesecake has chilled, make the whipped cream. Pour cream into a chilled mixing bowl. Using the wire whisk attachment of an electric mixer, whip the cream on medium speed until it begins to thicken. Drizzle in the honey and whip on medium-high speed until soft peaks form.

Top the cheesecake with the whipped cream, sprinkle with desired amount of the remaining ¹/₂ tablespoon of chia seeds, and garnish with Key lime slices. Cut cheesecake into 6 wedges and serve.

apricot hazelnut blondies

These blondies have a moist yet crumbly texture—I like to eat them slowly, with a fork, to savor the flavor. If possible, use organic or unsulfured apricots, which are not preserved with sulfur dioxide. You'll know them by their burnt orange color, a more natural hue than the bright orange of sulfur-treated apricots.

MAKES 16 BLONDIES

$1/2$ cup purified water

$1/4$ cup black or white chia seeds

6 tablespoons unsalted butter, melted

1 cup whole wheat pastry flour

$1/2$ teaspoon baking soda

$1/4$ teaspoon sea salt

$3/4$ cup firmly packed dark brown sugar

1 teaspoon pure vanilla extract

$1/4$ teaspoon pure almond extract

8 dried unsulfured Turkish apricots, extra thinly sliced

8 tablespoons chopped hazelnuts

In a liquid measuring cup or small bowl, whisk together the water and chia seeds and let stand for about 20 minutes. (Makes about $3/4$ cup extra-thick chia gel.)

Preheat the oven to 350°F.

Grease an 8-inch square nonstick (PFOA-free) baking pan with $1^{1}/_{2}$ teaspoons of the melted butter. Whisk together the flour, baking soda, and salt in a bowl and set aside. In a large bowl, with an electric mixer on low speed, mix together the remaining melted butter and brown sugar until well combined. Add the chia gel and vanilla and almond extracts and blend until thoroughly combined. Add the flour mixture and blend until just combined. Stir in the apricots and 6 tablespoons of the hazelnuts until evenly combined.

Pour into the prepared pan, spread evenly, and sprinkle with the remaining 2 tablespoons of hazelnuts. Bake until set and hazelnuts on top are lightly browned, about 28 minutes. Cool completely in the pan on a wire rack. Cut into 16 squares, carefully remove from pan, and serve. Store in an airtight container for up to 1 week in the refrigerator and up to 3 months in the freezer.

desserts, sweet nibbles, and cocktails

papaya, berry, and basil sorbet

What's especially nice about sorbet (aside from how yummy and refreshing it is) is that all you need is a food processor to make it—no fancy ice cream maker needed. Chia gel gives this papaya-berry-basil mix a decadent mouthfeel and helps keep it from becoming soupy as you eat it.

SERVES 4

¼ cup white chia seeds

¼ cup purified water

2 tablespoons freshly squeezed lemon juice (from about 1 small lemon)

3 tablespoons agave nectar or honey

6 ounces frozen papaya cubes (about 1 cup)

6 ounces frozen whole strawberries (about 1 cup)

1 teaspoon minced fresh basil

In a liquid measuring cup or small bowl, whisk together the chia seeds, water, and lemon juice and let stand for about 20 minutes. Stir in agave nectar. (Makes ¾ cup sweet lemon-chia gel.)

Remove the papaya and strawberries from the freezer and let stand for 15 minutes to just slightly thaw.

Place the papaya and strawberries in a food processor. Cover and pulse until well chopped. Add the sweet lemon-chia gel and puree until creamy. Add the basil and do a quick pulse to distribute. Serve immediately or place in an airtight container and store in the freezer for later.

chocolate chia–covered strawberries

If you have any leftover chocolate-chia mixture after dipping your straw-berries, quickly spoon it onto parchment paper and let cool. You can then break it up into pieces for a delicious chocolate "bark" similar to a Nestle's Crunch bar (only healthier and, to my mind, better tasting).

MAKES 8 STRAWBERRIES

8 large or extra-large strawberries with stems

4 ounces high-quality semisweet chocolate (about 60% cacao), chopped

2 tablespoons black or white chia seeds

Line a baking sheet with unbleached parchment. Place the strawberries on the baking sheet.

Slowly melt the chocolate in a double boiler over hot water, stirring only once or twice until completely melted and hot. Pour the chocolate into a teacup or small heatproof bowl and quickly whisk in the chia seeds.

Working very quickly, hold a strawberry by the stem and dunk about 3/4 of it into the melted chocolate to coat, allowing the excess to drip back into the teacup. Place back on the baking sheet and repeat with the remaining strawberries. Chill in the refrigerator until chocolate is set.

Serve at room temperature.

tart cherry–chia mimosa

Cocktails made with chia seeds are so gorgeous—between the seeds floating about and the rich color, they look eminently drinkable and festive for a celebration. This mimosa—which uses St. Germain, a sweet liqueur made from elderberry flowers—is no exception. Choose a tart cherry juice with no added sugar or flavorings (I like R. W. Knudsen Organic Just Tart Cherry Juice). Serve it in your best glassware and remember to stir the mimosas before serving!

-------------------------------- SERVES 4 --------------------------------

6 ounces (3/4 cup) 100% tart cherry juice

1 ounce (2 tablespoons) St. Germain

1 ounce (2 tablespoons) seltzer water or club soda

2 tablespoons black or white chia seeds

8 ounces (1 cup) Champagne or sparkling white wine, well chilled

In a large liquid measuring cup, whisk together the tart cherry juice, St. Germain, seltzer, and chia seeds and let stand for about 20 minutes. Chill well, then whisk again before using. (Makes about 1 1/8 cups cherry-chia gel.)

Pour the chilled cherry-chia gel into champagne flutes. Top with the Champagne and gently stir. Serve immediately along with a cocktail stirrer to evenly distribute chia as it's being enjoyed.

citrus pomegranate-peach margarita

I might not go as far as to call a margarita health food, but when you think about what's in this fruity take on the classic—chia with its many nutritious attributes, vitamin C–rich citrus, antioxidant-rich pomegranate juice, fiber-rich peaches—you can drink it without an ounce of guilt! This recipes calls for 6 ice cubes, but if you like a more potent drink just add 3.

SERVES 2

3 ounces (¼ cup plus 2 tablespoons) freshly squeezed clementine or tangerine juice (from about 2 clementines or tangerines)

2 ounces (¼ cup) 100% pomegranate juice

2 tablespoons white chia seeds

1 cup frozen peeled, sliced peaches or mango

¼ teaspoon sea salt

3 ounces (¼ cup plus 2 tablespoons) silver (blanco) 100% agave tequila

1 ounce (2 tablespoons) Cointreau

1 ounce (2 tablespoons) freshly squeezed lime juice (from about 1 lime) plus 2 thin lime slices

6 large ice cubes

In a liquid measuring cup, whisk together the clementine juice, pomegranate juice, and chia seeds and let stand for about 20 minutes. (Makes ⅔ cup citrus-pomegranate chia gel.)

Place the citrus-pom chia gel, frozen peaches, salt, tequila, Cointreau, lime juice, and ice cubes in a blender. Cover and puree well.

Pour into two chilled margarita or other large cocktail glasses and garnish with lime slices. Serve immediately.

spiked blueberry chia fizz

Anyone remember phosphates, an old soda fountain favorite? This blueberry fizz spiked with vodka tastes like a very grown-up version. It calls for the same blueberry compote used to make the yogurt parfaits (page 57).

SERVES 2

3 ounces (¼ cup plus
2 tablespoons) 80-proof
lemon or citrus vodka

4 ounces (½ cup) seltzer water
or club soda

¼ cup blueberry compote
(see page 57)

Fill two short cocktail glasses with ice. Divide the vodka between them, then top off each with seltzer water. Add a dollop of blueberry compote to each glass.

Serve with a short straw.

heirloom bloody mary

I've always thought that the Bloody Mary cocktail had great potential, but too often it's made with canned tomato juice and not enough spice. This fresh take on the original showcases those incredible heirloom tomatoes you can find at farmers' markets, blending them with vodka (small-batch organic is nice if you have it) and three kinds of heat. (For a milder Mary halve the horseradish, cayenne, and hot sauce.) This is a perfect addition to a summertime brunch.

SERVES 2

2 teaspoons black or white chia seeds

¼ cup purified water

Kosher salt, for garnishing rims

Freshly ground black pepper, for garnishing rims (optional)

2 large ripe heirloom tomatoes

1 teaspoon sea salt

½ small cucumber, peeled and coarsely chopped

1 ounce (2 tablespoons) freshly squeezed lime juice (from 1 lime)

3 ounces (¼ cup plus 2 table-spoons) 80-proof vodka

2 teaspoons prepared or fresh grated horseradish

½ teaspoon celery seed

½ teaspoon ground cayenne

Dash of Bragg's liquid aminos or coconut aminos

3 to 4 dashes hot pepper sauce

Pickled asparagus spears or green beans, for garnish

Celery stalks, for garnish

In a liquid measuring cup or small bowl, whisk together the chia seeds and water and let stand for about 20 minutes. (Makes about ¼ cup chia gel.)

Take two highball glasses and wet the rims. Coat the rims in the kosher salt mixed with black pepper. Set aside.

Core and dice the tomatoes, reserving all juices and seeds in a bowl. Toss the tomatoes with sea salt and set aside for 10 to 15 minutes to let the salt draw the juices out.

Place the chia gel, tomato mixture, cucumber, lime juice, vodka, horseradish, celery seed, cayenne, aminos, and hot sauce in a blender. Pulse until coarsely chopped, then blend on high until liquefied.

Add ice to each glass and divide the Bloody Mary between the glasses. Garnish with asparagus spears and celery stalks and serve.

vegetable garden-to-table mojito

Mojitos are a Latin favorite that typically get their flavor from mint and lime juice. Here I've added to the mix with carrot juice and ginger ale. And while you might not ordinarily think of drinks as providing fiber, this one will actually add a little to your day's intake.

-------------------------- SERVES 2 --------------------------

1 cup 100% pure pressed carrot juice

2 tablespoons black or white chia seeds

1 cup peeled, chopped, seeded cucumber

2 tablespoons fresh mint leaves

3 ounces (1/4 cup plus 2 tablespoons) 80-proof white rum

1 tablespoon honey or agave nectar

1/3 ounce (2 teaspoons) fresh lime juice

4 ounces (1/2 cup) ginger ale with fresh ginger

Chill two pilsner glasses or large goblets.

In a large liquid measuring cup, whisk together the carrot juice and chia seeds and let stand for about 20 minutes. (Makes about 1 1/8 cups carrot-chia gel.)

Place the cucumber, mint, rum, honey, lime juice, 1/4 cup of the ginger ale, 2 large ice cubes, and the carrot-chia gel in a blender. Cover and puree until smooth.

Pour into the chilled glasses, top with the remaining 1/4 cup of ginger ale, and serve immediately.

about the author

Janie Hoffman is the founder and CEO of Mamma Chia (www.mammachia.com), an organic line of chia-based foods and beverages. Janie developed the concept behind her company in the kitchen on her small avocado farm just outside San Diego, California. After incorporating chia into her diet to improve her own health, she experienced new levels of well-being and vitality that ultimately inspired the founding of Mamma Chia.

Leading beverage industry authority BevNET gave Mamma Chia's bottled drinks the 2011 award for best non-carbonated beverage and, in 2012, named Hoffman Person of the Year. A charismatic entrepreneur, Hoffman has quickly become a leader in the natural foods industry, and has been featured in the *New York Times*, *O* magazine, *Everyday with Rachel Ray*, *Details*, *Vogue*, *Real Simple*, *Prevention*, *Glamour*, the *Huffington Post*, the *Today* show, CBS, FOX News, and NBC News. Mamma Chia products are sold in stores across the country, ranging from Whole Foods to Safeway and Costco. Determined to share the magic of chia with as many people as possible, Janie's first book, *Chia Vitality: 30 Days to Better Health, Greater Vibrancy, and a More Meaningful and Purposeful Life*, was published in April 2014 by Harmony Books.

- - - - -

index

- - - - -